IMAGES
of America

SPORT FISHING
ON THE
OUTER BANKS

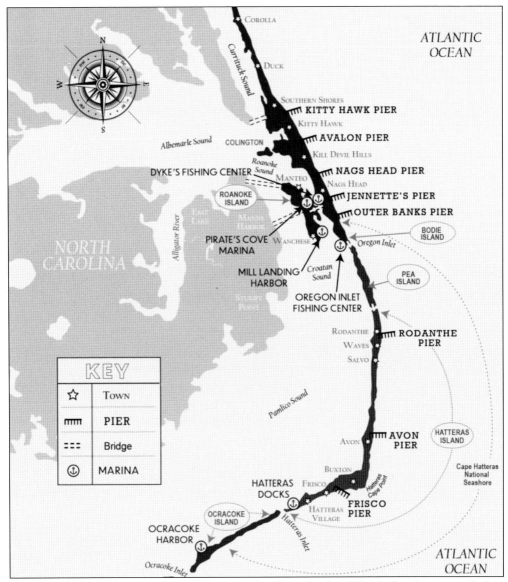

Sport fishermen have been making their way to the Outer Banks of North Carolina since the late 1800s to fish in an untouched landscape. These days, there are plenty of ways to fish, whether it is from the surf, a pier, a bridge, or one's boat. For the big-game angler, there are many marinas filled with boats to charter to Gulf Stream waters and dream trophies. (Courtesy of Coastal Impressions.)

ON THE COVER: Willie Etheridge Jr. (right) was considered by his peers to be the best fisherman on the Outer Banks. In the 1940s, Etheridge returned to Dyke's Fishing Center with a catch of channel bass and a group of satisfied anglers. Captain Will held the distinction of catching the first blue marlin brought to Oregon Inlet Fishing Center in 1953. (Courtesy of Willie Etheridge III.)

IMAGES
of America

SPORT FISHING
ON THE
OUTER BANKS

R. Wayne Gray and Nancy Beach Gray

ARCADIA
PUBLISHING

Published by Arcadia Publishing
Charleston, South Carolina

Printed in the United States of America

Library of Congress Control Number: 2023931344

For all general information, please contact Arcadia Publishing:
Telephone 843-853-2070
Fax 843-853-0044
E-mail sales@arcadiapublishing.com
For customer service and orders:
Toll-Free 1-888-313-2665

Visit us on the Internet at www.arcadiapublishing.com

In 1986, twelve-year-old Keil Gray cranks on the reel while her dad, coauthor R. Wayne Gray, holds the rod steady. When leaving Pirate's Cove Marina that early morning, they had to go around Roanoke Island to reach Oregon Inlet because the Washington Baum drawbridge was broken. It had been a rough ride out to the Gulf Stream, in which most of the party became seasick. They were fishing for dolphin and tuna aboard the *Free Agent* with Capt. Rick Caton. (Courtesy of R. Wayne Gray.)

CONTENTS

ACKNOWLEDGMENTS

I am grateful that my coauthor and late husband, R. Wayne Gray, left me with a contract and an outline for *Sport Fishing on the Outer Banks*. He instilled in me a love for local history and a feeling of urgency to record it before it is lost. I rode on the coattails of his big personality when making contacts and conducting research.

My deepest gratitude goes to our longtime editor, Caitrin Cunningham, and the team at Arcadia Publishing for trusting me to finish. Jami Lanier of the National Park Service and Tama Creef and Stuart Parks of the Outer Banks History Center have always gone the extra mile for me. Daryl Law of Jennette's Pier was gracious to share his files.

The stories, photographs, and historical facts that local families give to me are the lifeblood of this book. I am ever amazed at how generous people are with their time and family treasures. The photograph courtesy lines reflect how many folks helped me. Deanie Midgett, Rita Lewark Pledger, and Spurgeon Stowe deserve a special mention. I do not know where I would be without Billy Carl Tillett who identified faces, boats, and fish species while clarifying how things used to be done.

At the writing of this book, there were a few men still working like Tony Tillett and Dean Johnson who experienced the discovery of new and exciting fisheries on the Outer Banks. I conducted many interviews with the next generations of these pioneers. I am indebted to Joanne Baum Clift, Willie Etheridge III, and "Little Edgar" Styron.

Author Molly Harrison generously read over the final draft for grammatical and historical accuracy.

I am thankful for local authors whose writings gave me a solid background. The research paper preserving early sport fishing history by Suzanne Godley and Brian Edwards is a gem. Last but not least, I am grateful to Aycock Brown, who, while promoting the Outer Banks as a vacation destination, unwittingly preserved sport fishing history.

Many images in this book appear courtesy of the Outer Banks History Center (OBHC); the National Park Service, Cape Hatteras National Seashore (NPS, CHNS); and coauthor Richard Wayne Gray (RWG).

INTRODUCTION

Fishing methods have not changed significantly since humans caught the first fish. The atavistic thrill of a fish tugging on the other end of a line remains the same today as it did for the Indigenous people and for the English settlers who came to the Outer Banks of North Carolina in the mid-1660s.

One thing that has changed is the ways devised to get to where the fish are. It used to be that unless a recreational fisherman had a boat, he had to stand on a canal bank, on the sound's edge, or in the surf to get close to fishing grounds. Now, fishermen can walk over the breakers on any of the seven recreational fishing piers from Kitty Hawk to Avon. They can cast from catwalks attached to bridges spanning inlets and sounds. Boats and guides can be hired for inshore fishing in sounds, or fishermen can trailer their boats and put them in the water from many public boat ramps. Offshore trips to the beautiful Gulf Stream that flows past the North Carolina coast will yield catches of large game fish like wahoo, dolphin, or tuna. The most adventuresome anglers can engage in the ultimate battle of man against beast by going after the royalty of fish, the blue marlin.

The Outer Banks of North Carolina is a true fishermen's paradise. The US Congress created Cape Hatteras National Seashore in 1937 and preserved miles of oceanfront as a wild space. Local people originally resented the government for forcing them to sell their land, but later generations are grateful for areas where modern development is prohibited.

The earlier inhabitants of these barrier islands took no time for recreational fishing. They historically fished with nets to feed their families or sell their catches for shipment to northern markets. Soon, local people realized they had a commodity that other people would pay for—the opportunity to fish recreationally in a pristine environment—and that they could capitalize on that as a new source of income. Local men became guides, taking visitors to the spots where they knew fish were sure to bite. Oftentimes, a visiting angler would stay in the guide's home and eat at the family table. Having just one boat, the fishermen would transform their workboats into charter boats for the brief summer season.

As the need became clearer to make conditions more accommodating for paying parties, guides started building their own boats exclusively for charter purposes. Using their awareness of how a boat must perform in rough water and relying on a generational knowledge of boatbuilding, they created a new type of boat: the Carolina flare sportfisher.

In the late 1930s, fishing guides ventured farther and farther into the ocean. Out-of-state recreational fishermen came to Hatteras because of its proximity to the Gulf Stream, the warm-water current 30 miles offshore. These fishermen hired local captains and mates to help them get to bountiful fishing grounds, of which natives were previously unaware. During the era from the Revolutionary War to after the Civil War, Outer Banks inhabitants took advantage of the swift-moving current as they piloted schooners to the West Indies to trade lumber for rum and molasses. Their descendants became fishermen and stayed closer to home. They did not view the Gulf Stream as a reasonable place to fish.

New Jersey angler Hugo Rutherford caught the first blue marlin brought to the Hatteras docks in 1938. Rutherford and other northern fishermen taught Hatterasmen how to rig up and fish for big game like tuna, sailfish, and white and blue marlin. Local fishermen caught the big-game fever, and before long they were taking their own parties to fish for ultimate trophies. Although World War II caused a brief cessation of sport fishing, after the war captains were soon back to the offshore obsession. With only basic instrumentation and a strong understanding of weather signs, these pioneers of Gulf Stream fishing bravely headed out to sea daily, depending on each other and the Almighty for protection.

Cape Hatteras National Seashore promoted recreational fishing among US citizens. As part of that vision, a National Park Service concession site, Oregon Inlet Fishing Center, became a small but very busy harbor where visitors could charter a boat to fish inshore or offshore. Hundreds of onlookers gathered there on summer afternoons to watch the beautiful sport fishing boats return to the docks with their varied catches and sunburned clients. When the opportunity presented itself, a group of charter captains formed a corporation and won the concession contract for Oregon Inlet Fishing Center, a contract they held for 50 years.

Fishing has been one of the attractions that helped shape the Outer Banks into a premier tourist destination. As more visitors came to the Outer Banks to fish, the locals constructed tourist homes, hotels, and cottage courts to house them. Recreational fishermen brought their families to the area to eat in restaurants, buy souvenirs from gift shops, and play rounds of miniature golf. Surf fishing tournaments were organized and helped to extend the lucrative tourist season into autumn. Offshore fishing tournaments draw big boats and big money from all over the world to humble Outer Banks harbors. Hatteras holds on to the title of "Billfish Capital of the World," which was won in a formal competition with Puerto Rico in 1961.

Whether white perch fishing with a cane pole in a canal, dropping a line from a kayak, surf fishing in solitude, angling with the brotherhood of pier fishermen, or steaming to the Gulf Stream in a high-tech yacht, recreational fishing from the barrier islands is a joy and pleasure to thousands of anglers every year. Sport fishing continues to evolve. Guides offer new and exciting experiences of fly-fishing, spearfishing, and shrimping and crabbing excursions. Fishermen have become more ecologically minded and practice catch-and-release methods unless they want to eat their prize. These days, a fishing license must be obtained and kept at the ready.

For so many fishermen, the experience is about more than catching. It is about being content out on the water, being one with the beauty and serenity of nature. Recreational fishing has changed the face of the Outer Banks, greatly enhancing and powering its economy, creating a unique culture, and helping build its complex society.

In the 1920s, park Cape Hatteras National Seashore dreamer Frank Stick wrote in his book *The Call of the Surf*, "To feel the lift, the gentle mouthing, and then the irresistible tug and run of a 30-pound channel bass; to sense the jarring rush of the striper; to see the enormous length of a shark leave the waves in a headlong leap, while the line runs like water from your reel; these experiences are sufficient to send the blood pounding through the body, and to lift the sportsman into the ultimate heaven of happiness."

Some things have not changed.

One

A FISHERMAN'S PARADISE

David Stick (left) and Tommy Fearing (right) cannot keep from grinning after spearing two huge sheepsheads in 1935. They showed off their skills in a sport new to the Outer Banks: goggle fishing. Stick and Fearing, who held their own goggle fishing tournament complete with trophies, pose before one of the many shipwrecks that were fixtures on the Nags Head beach in those days. (Maud Hayes Stick Papers, OBHC.)

The first Outer Banks villages were built on the sound side, which offers protection from harsh ocean elements. Oceanfront property was considered to be wasteland, only suitable for grazing livestock. Tourists in the late 1800s and early 1900s stayed in sound-side accommodations. The beach was unwelcoming, with ghostly shipwrecks and remnants of ancient forests in the wash. (NPS, CHNS.)

After the Civil War, lifesaving service stations were built approximately every six miles along the coast of North Carolina in response to a high volume of shipwrecks. The stations hired local men to work as lifesaving surfmen. Small communities sprang up near the stations as surfmen's families settled nearby. Local families fished with nets for their daily food. Little boys or relaxed visitors were the only ones who fished with rod and reel for pleasure. (Maud Hayes Stick Papers, OBHC.)

As a young couple, Mattie and Jethro Midgett Sr. saw that the future of tourism was shifting from the sound side to the oceanfront. Well-to-do families from inland North Carolina farming communities were building cedar-shake cottages along the oceanfront. The Midgetts moved their home, shown here, and their grocery store from Nags Head Woods across the expanse of sand to the beach. (Jeffrey G. Midgett.)

In the 1930s, Dr. Herbert Dillon Walker took a break from his practice in Elizabeth City and was rewarded by this channel bass surf catch. He owned a cottage on the sound side in Nags Head. His daughter Edla married into the Foreman family who owned an oceanfront cottage built in 1916. The cottage, part of the group known as the Unpainted Aristocracy, still stands regally and is still owned by the Wood and Foreman families. (Foreman family.)

Tourists who came to Nags Head had to love fishing, swimming, and playing in the breakers like Jethro Midgett Jr. and his friends in 1940. There was not much else to do or see, but local and state politicians worked to change that. The Wright Brothers National Memorial located in Kill Devil Hills opened in 1932. *The Lost Colony*, an annual homespun pageant, became a symphonic drama and premiered at Roanoke Island's Waterside Theatre in 1937. (Jeffrey G. Midgett.)

North Carolina General Assembly representative R. Bruce Etheridge promoted Dare County far and wide by sending photographs like this one to fellow politicians to drool over. He was seeking funding for infrastructure like bridges and paved roads. "Outer Banks" is a relatively new branding term. On old seafaring maps, the North Carolina island strand was described as sand banks or sea banks. (Betty Bruce Stratton.)

This angler was a guest at the private home now known as Whalehead in Corolla. Before World War II, "Nags Head" was used loosely to designate the Outer Banks from south of the Virginia line to Oregon Inlet, and "the Banks" was used to delineate the area from Oregon Inlet to Ocracoke Island. The fledging Manteo Tourist Bureau used the terms "Dare Beaches" and "the Sir Walter Raleigh Coast Land" in promotional newspaper advertisements. (Whalehead.)

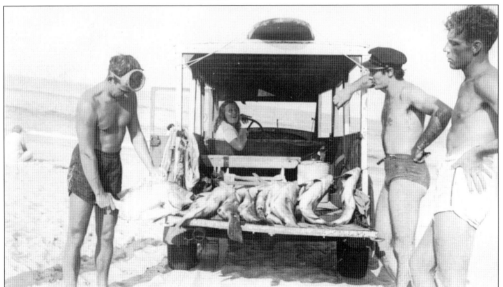

Ready for any kind of action, this beach cruising jalopy was outfitted with a college flag, an extra gas can, a wooden surfboard, spears for goggle fishing, and a great catch of the day. Native Tommy Fearing is wearing the captain's hat. Visitors were using the beach as a playground, and locals were beginning to see the possibilities for making a better living for their families by capitalizing on that. (Maud Hayes Stick Papers, OBHC.)

Looking self-assured, David Stick casually held his prize from goggle fishing on September 2, 1938, in Nags Head. His father, wildlife artist Frank Stick, moved the family from New Jersey to tiny Skyco village on Roanoke Island in 1929. Frank Stick honed in on the incredible natural beauty of the Outer Banks. He became a real estate developer and mindfully developed Southern Shores. (Maud Hayes Stick Papers, OBHC.)

Just as goggles help a fisherman to clearly see underwater, Frank Stick's perspective helped local people see the wonder and potential of their untouched paradise. One of his many groundbreaking conservationist ideas was the establishment of Cape Hatteras National Seashore. It sparked great controversy at first, but later generations have come to see the value of preserving a large stretch of undeveloped coastline. (Maud Hayes Stick Papers, OBHC.)

In the early 1960s, Charlie Brown leans against the dock pilings in mainland Manns Harbor. The net houses of commercial fishermen lined the ditch where the men moored their workboats. Before Charlie was born, commercial fishing was the driving force of the area's economy. In his lifetime, sport fishing became dominant, and Charlie was a participant as a charter captain and mate. (Nettie Brown Tisch.)

Standing by a whale skeleton meant to attract tourists to the family's Esso station in Nags Head were, from left to right, Charles, Oscar, and Earl Ray Midgett. It was a key spot where the roads to Roanoke Island and the northern and southern banks intersected, soon nicknamed Whalebone Junction. Charles Midgett would grow up to be a respected captain who drove through Whalebone Junction daily on his way to his charter boat. (NPS, CHNS.)

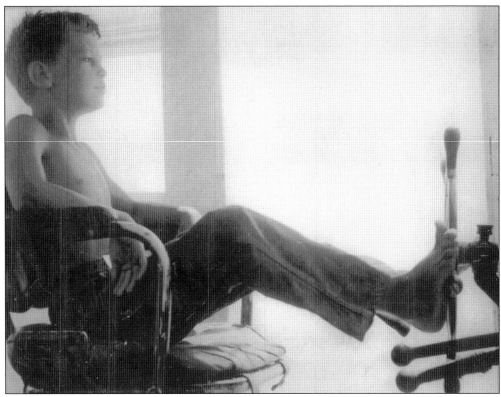

Tony Tillett was born into a fishing family and was raised near Whalebone Junction. His father, Sambo Tillett, opened Sam and Omie's as a place where fishermen could get an early breakfast and charter a boat. Tony took parties out on his own when he was 12 years old accompanied by a mate who was also 12. One surprised foreign tourist kept asking, "Where is Cap-ee-tan?" until he realized that the boy standing before him was the skipper. (Tony Tillett.)

In the 1930s, Wayland Baum and his son Billy could not have imagined that taking out (or "carrying out," as locals say) parties to fish in the Croatan Sound in the 1930s would lead to today's chartered Gulf Stream trips on multimillion-dollar sport fishing vessels. For the Baums, the early years yielded meager wages supplemented by boarding fishermen in their home for $1.50 per day and 50¢ per meal. (Joanne Baum Clift.)

Tourism experienced a significant jump as bridges and roadways improved. In 1959, Billy Holton fishes at Dyke's Fishing Center next to the Washington Baum Bridge that connected Roanoke Island to Nags Head. Holton became a captain who built his own boats for his charter business. His boatbuilding evolved to the point that he established Holton Custom Yachts, where he constructed luxury showpiece sport fishing vessels for others. (Tammy Holton Jennings.)

In Outer Banks villages, where everyone knew each other or was related, children had a lot of freedom to roam and explore. Boys learned the ways of the water and how to handle boats by helping their male relatives at an early age. In addition to fishermen, the area has produced many Merchant Marines and Coast Guardsmen. These Cape Hatteras boys were rescuing fish from a dried-up pond in 1959. (NPS, CHNS.)

Manteo High School students Ken Mann (left) and David O'Neal (right) spread out their catch on the low wall that bordered the Tourist Bureau in 1974. Bureau chief Aycock Brown never tired of getting shots of happy anglers and their fish. At that age while in a boat, Mann would often pantomime having a huge fish on his line for startled passengers watching from cars crossing a bridge. (Aycock Brown Collection, Ken Mann.)

These friends, who also taught together in Manteo schools, rode on the beach looking for fish in 1973. They got this huge haul without ever using a fishing pole when big bluefish drove frightened trout up on the shore. All they had to do was pick them up. Pictured are, from left to right, (first row) R. Wayne Gray, George Pearce, Lionel Shannon Jr., and "Little Jeffrey" Midgett; (second row) R.V. Owens, Andy Meekins, Robert Midgette, and Jeffrey Midgett. (Aycock Brown Collection, RWG.)

Two

PUTTING THE OUTER BANKS ON THE MAP

In the days before specialized fishing clothing, these anglers waded into the surf in their street clothes at Cape Point off Buxton on Hatteras Island. When channel bass are running, the call must be answered immediately. Cape Point is the premier fishing spot because it elbows into the migratory fish routes of the Atlantic about 30 miles from the mainland. (D. Victor Meekins Collection, OBHC.)

Described as sticking out like a sore thumb, Cape Point is situated near where the southern warmer waters of the Gulf Stream intersect with the northern colder waters of the Labrador Current. This collision creates shifting sand bars that are a gathering spot for a variety of saltwater fish. Cape Point also features beaches that face north and south. The south beach is a good spot for gathering shells. (NPS, CHNS.)

The unpredictable sand shoals and rough conditions that make for good fishing are hazardous to oceangoing vessels. That is why this area has been known as the Graveyard of the Atlantic for centuries. In this July 1963 photograph, visitors fish from the shipwreck *Altoona* at Cape Point. These days, a permit is required for driving on the beach along this stretch of Cape Hatteras National Seashore. (NPS, CHNS.)

Another draw for fishermen is Oregon Inlet, the treacherous waterway where ocean waters cut into the barrier island to reach sound waters. In the 1990s, two surf fishermen in waders walk past a modern shipwreck. Several boys investigate the rigging of the *Lois Joyce*, a commercial trawler that ran aground during a storm in December 1982. (Drew Wilson Collection, OBHC.)

Frank Stick, a wildlife artist, engineer, and builder, was able to garner support for his idea of preserving part of the coastland of the Outer Banks for future generations. The US Congress authorized the formation of the nation's first national seashore park from south Nags Head to Ocracoke in August 1937. Due to World War II, land acquisition delays, and other setbacks, Cape Hatteras National Seashore was not officially established until 1953. (OBHC.)

The creation of Cape Hatteras National Seashore coincided with the inception of other government programs, the Works Progress Administration (WPA) and the Civilian Conservation Corps (CCC). WPA and CCC laborers, usually unattached and unemployed men, were brought to the area to build sand fences that created sand dunes. In 1936, WPA men in Buxton on Hatteras Island sat long enough for a photograph. (NPS, CHNS.)

The coastal park plan included the construction of wall-like dunes to protect the lives and property of residents on the Outer Banks from ocean overwash. Many locals did not agree with creating dunes and held to the idea that floodwaters needed to sweep over the barrier island and then recede unimpeded. A WPA crew constructed a fence to trap sand and establish dunes in 1936. (NPS, CHNS.)

WPA and CCC men planted beach grass during the late 1930s in hopes that vegetation would help hold sand in place; however, today's geologists identify the Outer Banks as a migrating sandbar. Planners of Cape Hatteras National Seashore recognized the value of a coastal highway as a way for tourists to safely and easily access the public park. In 1952, a new paved road to Hatteras was completed. (NPS, CHNS.)

Needed most of all was a bridge to span Oregon Inlet and connect Nags Head on Bodie Island to Pea Island and the chain of villages on Hatteras Island. Politicians were introduced to the newest national park and wooed by an offshore trip to the Gulf Stream in June 1957. From left are Governors Freeman (Minnesota), Davis (North Carolina), Foss (South Dakota), O'Neal (Ohio), and McNichols (Colorado), who hold their catches on the Hatteras dock. (NPS, CHNS.)

Before the bridge was built, residents and visitors had to cross Oregon Inlet by ferryboat. Shown here in 1941 is the *Barcelona*, owned and captained by Toby Tillett, which made daily journeys between Bodie and Pea Islands for 25 years until the state took over the operation. Early sport fishermen had a ferry ride and a bumpy car ride along sand ruts before arriving in Hatteras—all part of the adventure. (D. Victor Meekins Collection, OBHC.)

The steel construction of this Ocracoke ferry in 1959 reflected the state's commitment to the ferry system. To this day, Ocracoke Island residents depend on ferries to bring tourists to the farthest section of Cape Hatteras National Seashore. Visitors can feel the freedom of disconnecting from the outside world as they follow the national seashore to its southern border. (NPS, CHNS.)

The bridge stretching over Oregon Inlet completed the coastal highway and made most of Cape Hatteras National Seashore accessible to all citizens. The Herbert C. Bonner Bridge was named for a North Carolina representative who brokered the deal between the federal National Park Service and the state. The bridge was 2.7 miles long and opened in 1963. (NPS, CHNS.)

The description accompanying this 1965 photograph reflected the disgust of the National Park Service employee who wrote it: "Uncontrolled, unsafe, and unauthorized parking by fisherman." The fishermen who left their vehicles on the shoulders of the road so they could get to the catwalk running along the south side of the Bonner Bridge undoubtedly felt that it was worth the risk of getting in trouble. (NPS, CHNS.)

In October 1990, from left to right, out-of-town fishermen James Richart, Dewey Frye, and James Shive got extensions on their vacations when a 370-foot section of the Bonner Bridge collapsed into Oregon Inlet. An unsecured dredge hit the span during a nor'easter. The men who were stranded on Hatteras Island without telephone or electric services were undeterred in their fishing pursuits. (Drew Wilson Collection, OBHC.)

In 1963, Americans were taking to the road and discovering their nation. The Cape Hatteras National Seashore campground at Oregon Inlet had ocean, sound, and bridge views. Oftentimes, overflow crowds camped four miles north at the Coquina Beach access or across the bridge at the old ferry slip. In this photograph, a modern comfort station is located in the midst of the tents and camper trailers. (NPS, CHNS.)

Surf fishing and Cape Hatteras National Seashore have gone hand in hand since the park's beginning. In 1967, Rudy Gray demonstrated surf fishing in Rodanthe while photographer Aycock Brown took shots for a promotional magazine. Even though the picture was staged, there was no doubt that Gray, a diehard fisherman, was trying for an actual bite and landing. (Aycock Brown Collection, OBHC.)

Bob Preston (right) relocated from Norfolk to Nags Head after retiring from the US Army in 1957. To live on the Outer Banks, often residents had to work several jobs to make ends meet. Preston sold real estate, but his real passion was working as a fishing guide. He was pictured with Bob Pond (left) who came to test the Striper Swipers fishing lures that he invented. Apparently, they worked. (Pat Preston.)

The Preston family (from left to right are Stuart, Pat, Bob, and Elnora) took a busman's holiday as they enjoyed a family fishing trip in 1964. Bob converted a Jeep into a beach buggy that he used for driving on the shore when acting as a surf-fishing guide. Daughter Stuart looked for soft sand fleas to use as bait. Bookings for the guide business were taken at the Carolinian Hotel. (Pat Preston.)

In 1964, the Preston family stopped in front of the wreck of the *Richmond* in Salvo. Bob Preston founded the Beach Buggy Association in 1967 when the National Park Service announced that all beaches would be closed to vehicular traffic. Money raised through the association was used to send Preston to Washington, DC, to lobby against the decision. North Carolina's US senator Walter B. Jones Sr. was most helpful in keeping beaches open. (Pat Preston.)

In 1990, two off-duty policemen from Fairfax County, Virginia, Marc Sturdivant (left) and David Kuhar (right), swing their legs from the tailgate of a pickup as they waited for a bite at Oregon Inlet. Being able to drive on the beach and claim a spot for the day is part of the ritual of surf fishing. One of the policemen explained, "This is the way we relax. We're just stressed out, you know." (Drew Wilson Collection, OBHC.)

Aspiring anglers attentively watched Ken Lauer in the early 1970s as he instructed them during the Fish With A Ranger program. Former Cape Hatteras National Seashore superintendent Tom Hartman said, "To many of the participants, this fishing program is the first time they have held a rod and reel. This experience which they have with the resource and equipment may mold behaviors that will last the rest of their lives." (NPS, CHNS.)

Angling clubs were formed to promote friendly competition over the years. Award banquets that were held after the conclusion of tournaments were elegant events, something unusual for beach culture. In 1978, Chuck Higgins of Elizabeth City proudly holds a winner's trophy while wearing his fishing regalia jacket with embroidered patches and buttons denoting club memberships. (Foreman family.)

Queenie James (left) was a longtime employee and friend of John Wood Foreman (right). She would come with the family from Elizabeth City to the Wood Foreman home, one of the Unpainted Aristocracy houses, in the Nags Head Beach Cottages Historic District. Other homeowners along that stretch of beach would have their binoculars trained on James. If she were out fishing, others would follow suit. James led the pack. (Foreman family.)

Three

WALKING THE PLANKS

The action was heavy on the north side of Jennette's Fishing Pier on this 1950s day. Lines may tangle and special vantage points may be lost, but friendliness and camaraderie prevail among pier fishermen. Pier anglers will jump in to help a novice fisherman land a fish and then congratulate that person as if he did it all himself. (Jennette's Pier.)

Bill Jennette Sr. always wanted to own a fishing pier and set his sights on a former WPA camp and 570 feet of oceanfront at Whalebone Junction. Laborers had been housed there while building sand dunes in Nags Head. Bill came to the auction with only $2,000 cash and got the property unexpectedly when a man who won the bid backed out. He stood with his wife, Lina Belle Jennette, on opening day at Jennette's Pier in 1939. (Jennette's Pier.)

The T-shaped pier that Bill Jennette built with his family extended 740 feet into the Atlantic and rested on 65-foot-long sunken pilings. He invested another $6,000 into the pier and pier house. This photograph, taken from the pier house looking toward Roanoke Sound, shows two large WPA camp barracks that were later converted into apartments for tourists. The smaller building is a bathhouse with showers. (Jennette's Pier.)

JENNETTE'S FAMOUS FISHING PIER AND MOTOR COURT

This 1960s postcard shows the Jennette's Pier complex in a perfectly manicured state. It was a struggle to keep repairing and rebuilding Jennette's Pier, which repeatedly took massive hits from hurricanes and storms. Once in its history, the pier was pummeled by shipwrecked schooner, *Francis E. Waters*, which was drug up by a storm from the ocean floor where it had been since 1889 and hurled at the pier. (Jennette's Pier.)

The North Carolina Aquarium Society (NCAS) purchased Jennette's Pier in 2001, but before it could open, Hurricane Isabel shut it down. The nonprofit NCAS ran short of money, but the deep pockets of the state came to the rescue. In 2008, a tremendous pump was used to sink concrete pilings for a whole new Jennette's Pier, making it the oldest and youngest pier on the Outer Banks. (Jennette's Pier.)

Known as the finest trout fisherman to ever walk the beach, Lionel Shannon Sr. started every day that was "halfway fittin' to fish" at the Kitty Hawk Pier eating breakfast and drinking coffee until the sun came up. After an intense session of ribbing and telling yarns, he and a group of regulars would fan out looking for fishing holes while trying to keep them a secret. (Barry Shannon.)

Lionel Shannon Sr. liked his speckled trout fried, eating the head, eyes, and even the crunchy tail. After he and his wife, Melba (or "Mebs"), sold the Sea Kove Motel in Kitty Hawk in 1976, they racked up 20 good years of fishing. Whenever Shannon was dragging and blue, it meant that Mebs had outfished him. Besides Mebs, Shannon sought to beat Nags Head surf-fishing guide Bob Preston. (Jim Bunch photograph; Barry Shannon.)

Brian Horsley (left), a self-described pier rat, grew us admiring Lionel Shannon Sr. and another Kitty Hawk Pier icon, retired game warden Preston Barber. Horsley learned much from the men about fishing and, more importantly, about life. He eventually found his real calling as a fly-fishing guide out of Oregon Inlet, working with his wife, Sarah Gardner, and chasing fish all over the western hemisphere. (Brian Horsley.)

Two tough souls clean their fish on the Avalon Pier in Kill Devil Hills in 1987. The heavy surf was a result of a tropical storm that was making its way out to sea. The Avalon Pier was built in 1958 and has taken its share of beatings, most recently losing 220 feet to Hurricane Dorian in 2019. Fans of the vintage structure enjoy arcade games and a two-story food and bar area. (Drew Wilson Collection, OBHC.)

B.T. Smith (right) of New Kent, Virginia, beams after his unusual catch of a 40-pound citation sailfish off the end of Avalon Pier in the 1990s. Sailfish are normally found miles offshore in warmer Gulf Stream waters. Local fishermen Sonny Macaranas (left) of Kill Devil Hills and Romeo Malana (center) of Moyock helped by gaffing the billfish. (Drew Wilson Collection, OBHC.)

Holding down a pier corner while waiting for a bite, a snoozing couple shares a pillow in the 1990s. The Nags Head Fishing Pier was built in 1947, and shortly after that Mann's Recreation Center opened next door with a roller-skating rink and duckpin bowling. In the 1970s, the complex became the Footsball Palace, an arcade hot spot for teenagers, and the Atlantis, a nightclub for an older crowd. (Drew Wilson Collection, OBHC.)

In the 1970s, Rick Tupper shows off his 11-pound, 12-ounce speckled trout. Since he was a frequenter of the Nags Head Fishing Pier, owner Joe Justice asked him to take a job as manager. To seal the deal, Justice pulled out a wad of cash and paid him in advance. Tupper also fished commercially while getting established in the local art scene. As a starving artist, he would catch a fish, use it as a model for painting, and then eat it. (Rick Tupper.)

Rick Tupper (left) fishes in the Nags Head Surf Fishing Tournament with teammate Todd Hayman in the early 2000s. About Tupper's uncanny fishing ability, his wife, Didi Tupper, recalled, "Rick would walk down the Oregon Inlet Bridge catwalk past all the fishermen lined up there. He carried only the simple rod that he had for 40 years—no gizmos, no special bait. In a short time he got his limit and quietly made his way back past those same unlucky fishermen." (Rick Tupper.)

After being burned in a welding accident, Edward "Red" Mitchell moved from West Virginia to the beach. He was inspired to construct the Seaport Fishing Pier in South Nags Head in 1958 by his wife, Pat, who loved to fish. Here, Red holds a sturgeon in the store section of the pier house that also contained an apartment for his family. Along with the pier, he built all of the adjoining rental houses and apartments. (Juanita Mitchell Wescott.)

In 1962, the Ash Wednesday Storm took out most of the Seaport Fishing Pier. An eyewitness saw the pier house "explode," and all of the Mitchells' possessions were lost as ocean overwash swept the beach clean. A young scientist, Bob Dolan, had a research trailer on the pier full of technical equipment for measuring waves. Dolan took this photograph of Mitchell driving tide line stakes in preparation to rebuild. (Juanita Mitchell Wescott.)

With determination and a little hired help, Red Mitchell had the Seaport Fishing Pier ready to reopen in June 1962, just a few months after the Ash Wednesday Storm. This postcard, showing no trace of the devastating tidal storm, was taken about a year later. Mitchell died in 1969. His wife ran the pier for a season and then sold it to Garry Oliver, who renamed it the Outer Banks Fishing Pier. (Juanita Mitchell Wescott.)

Fishing piers on the Outer Banks gave out complimentary tide charts, newly printed each year. Times for low and high tides for April through November were listed for serious anglers. The inside covers of this chart given out by the Seaport Fishing Pier had illustrations of commonly caught fish. Tide charts were essential for every tackle box. (Juanita Mitchell Wescott.)

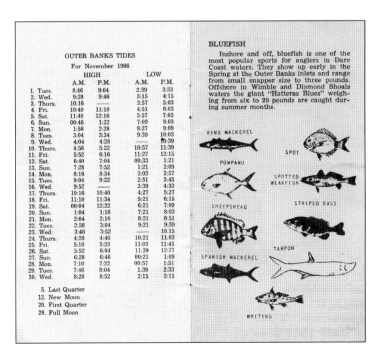

OUTER BANKS TIDES

For November 1966

		HIGH		LOW	
		A.M.	P.M.	A.M.	P.M.
1.	Tues.	8:46	9:04	2:39	3:33
2.	Wed.	9:28	9:46	3:15	4:15
3.	Thurs.	10:16	—	3:57	5:03
4.	Fri.	10:40	11:10	4:51	6:03
5.	Sat.	11:40	12:16	5:57	7:03
6.	Sun.	00:46	1:22	7:09	8:03
7.	Mon.	1:58	2:28	8:27	9:09
8.	Tues.	3:04	3:34	9:39	10:03
9.	Wed.	4:04	4:28	—	10:39
10.	Thurs.	4:58	5:22	10:57	11:39
11.	Fri.	5:52	6:16	11:27	12:15
12.	Sat.	6:40	7:04	00:33	1:21
13.	Sun.	7:28	7:52	1:21	2:09
14.	Mon.	8:16	8:34	2:03	2:57
15.	Tues.	9:04	9:22	2:51	3:45
16.	Wed.	9:52	—	3:39	4:33
17.	Thurs.	10:16	10:40	4:27	5:27
18.	Fri.	11:10	11:34	5:21	6:15
19.	Sat.	00:04	12:22	6:21	7:09
20.	Sun.	1:04	1:16	7:21	8:03
21.	Mon.	2:04	2:10	8:21	8:51
22.	Tues.	2:58	3:04	9:21	9:39
23.	Wed.	3:46	3:52	—	10:15
24.	Thurs.	4:28	4:40	10:21	11:03
25.	Fri.	5:10	5:22	11:03	11:45
26.	Sat.	5:52	6:04	11:39	12:27
27.	Sun.	6:28	6:46	00:21	1:09
28.	Mon.	7:10	7:22	00:57	1:51
29.	Tues.	7:46	8:04	1:39	2:33
30.	Wed.	8:28	8:52	2:15	3:15

5. Last Quarter
12. New Moon
20. First Quarter
28. Full Moon

BLUEFISH

Inshore and off, bluefish is one of the most popular sports for anglers in Dare Coast waters. They show up early in the Spring at the Outer Banks inlets and range from small snapper size to three pounds. Offshore in Wimble and Diamond Shoals waters the giant "Hatteras Blues" weighing from six to 20 pounds are caught during summer months.

KING MACKEREL

SPOT

POMPANO

SPOTTED WEAKFISH

SHEEPSHEAD

STRIPED BASS

TARPON

SPANISH MACKEREL

WHITING

Whalebone
North Carolina

This 1980s-era postcard shows an area that is not actually Whalebone, but South Nags Head. The picture must have been taken after a storm since the Outer Banks Fishing Pier has significant damage at its end, and the beach exhibits severe erosion. Pier owners face constant repair and maintenance bills, causing them to seek ways to bring in more income like opening pier bars and restaurants. (RWG.)

Part of establishing Cape Hatteras National Seashore was making provisions for concessions, a situation in which the National Park Service partners with private companies to bring services to the public. A unique park concession on the Outer Banks is a fishing pier. In this 1960 photograph, the 24-foot-wide, 820-foot-long Chicamacomico Fishing Pier pushed its way out into the Atlantic. It is now known as the Rodanthe Pier. (NPS, CHNS.)

A locked-up Rodanthe Pier house, a dusting of snow, and a lack of vehicles in this 1970s photograph all point to the quiet offseason that used to be part of the cycle of life on the Outer Banks. In 2008, the Rodanthe Fishing Pier got a moment in Hollywood's spotlight when it was featured in the movie *Nights in Rodanthe,* starring Richard Gere and Diane Lane. (NPS, CHNS.)

Two other concession piers were built on Cape Hatteras National Seashore property. The Frisco Pier or Cape Hatteras Fishing Pier opened in 1962. Its skeletal remains were removed in 2019. Hatteras Island's third and final pier, the Avon Fishing Pier, was built in 1964, the year after the Herbert C. Bonner Bridge over Oregon Inlet opened. Storms have pared its length down by half and have made the walk to the end a winding, rising, and falling journey. (NPS, CHNS.)

Outer Banks fishing piers have been a vital part of tournaments that raise money for good causes. In Dare County, the Lions Club has conducted its VIP Fishing Tournament for Visually Impaired Persons for decades. Mildred Barbee of Durham, North Carolina, joyously holds up a spot caught by a friend in October 1988 at the Nags Head Fishing Pier. (Drew Wilson Collection, OBHC.)

Since piers have limited life spans, some people fear that wooden piers will become things of the past. Piers are for more than just fishing. They are for admiring a brilliant sunrise, watching a migrating whale, making a quick friend, peeking between slats at crashing waves, strolling after supper, and even releasing a loved one's ashes into the swirling water. (Brian Horsley.)

Four

CARRYING OUT PARTIES

Wayland Baum was born across the sound seven months after the Wright brothers flew their heavier-than-air machine in Kitty Hawk. He held a variety of jobs, including delivering wood, coal, paint, and annual supplies to lighthouses from a side-wheel steamer. He made substantial money commercial fishing for shad before the Depression but continued to live frugally while wisely investing his nest egg. (Baum family.)

With limited ways to make a living, many Outer Bankers used their boats to take out hunting and fishing parties, depending on the seasons. In this 1941 photograph, a customer labeled as "Doc" shot standing from a sinkbox, a coffin-like structure with a surrounding platform, that Wayland Baum set up in the Pamlico Sound off Bodie Island Lighthouse. During the offseason, Baum made all of his own decoys. (Baum family.)

Wayland Baum kept commercial fishing boats on the west side of Wanchese at the end of Baum's ditch. He charter fished out of Tink Tillett's dock at Mill Landing Harbor on the east side. Baum, with his firm grip on the tiller, took early charter fishing parties inshore in the sound. Baum lived to be 103 and remembered that in the 1940s nobody knew that tuna and marlin were accessible offshore. (Baum family.)

Parties that went out with Wayland Baum came to fish, and creature comforts were not part of the deal. The thrifty Baum spent as little as possible, witnessed by the folding metal chairs seen in this photograph. His customers came from New York; Baltimore; Washington, DC; and Norfolk. Like these two anglers with a striped bass catch in 1941, the goal was to go home with meat to eat. (Baum family.)

In the 1940s, Capt. Wayland Baum took out a party of five Mennonites from Lynnhaven, Virginia. They caught 33 channel bass, but because of their beliefs, they would not have their photograph taken with the bounty. When they got to the dock, they loaded the fish in their Model T Ford (there was no ice available at the time) and piled in on top of the fish for the ride home. (Baum family.)

Wayland Baum was among a group of Outer Banks fishermen who saw charter fishing leap from a basic service to one of the top money-generating industries in North Carolina. When he foresaw the potential for growth, Baum upgraded to the party boat *Alethia*. Later, he purchased a Chris-Craft (shown here) and blended the names of two granddaughters to rename it the *Maranna*. (Baum family.)

An African proverb states, "When an old man dies, a library burns to the ground." The knowledge that Wayland Baum held about weather and nature was astounding. He knew everything from how to find a clam bed to how to predict the severity of a storm. For men of that era, reading signs of nature was essential for making a living and for protecting the lives of the people they took to sea. (Baum family.)

MANNS HARBOR MARINA

CAREDWYN
WANCHESE

The striped bass were biting off mainland Manns Harbor from where Jesse Etheridge (second from left) ran his boat in the fall. The fish display rack from the small marina in Manns Harbor was lifted into the *Caredwyn* for this photograph. His daughter Carrol Tillett recalled, "He was a good man, but he was high strung. People loved to listen to him, and he was always yackin' and hollerin'." (Robin Daniels Holt.)

Jesse Etheridge's son McRae "Mack" Etheridge stands at the front door of Mack's Fishing Center on Mill Landing Harbor in Wanchese. Mack set up a general store on the waterfront when he returned home after serving six years in the Coast Guard. As a devoted fisherman, he saw an opportunity to expand his business by renting wooden skiffs and tackle to tourists. (Randy O'Neal.)

In the 1960s, one of Mack Etheridge's rental boats pulls up to a primitive dock in Mill Landing Harbor. Mack rented rowboats for $2 and 20-foot juniper boats with 10-horsepower motors for $5. To keep visiting fishermen in the know, each boat had a metal plate bolted inside with an etched map on it with Xs marking the best fishing spots. (Robin Daniels Holt.)

This happy family stood with a huge flounder caught aboard one of Mack's boats. Mack further enlarged Mack's Fishing Center by adding a diner where a customer could get a full breakfast for 65¢ or a fried shrimp dinner for $1.25. During the winters, when business was slow, Mack wrote lyrics for a total of 80 songs. "Honey, Let's Go Fishing" was published by Nordike Songs and Music Company in 1962. (Randy O'Neal.)

This photograph taken inside the store at Mack's Fishing Center showed loads of inventory, everything from gas cans to rods and reels. It was also a place to sit in a rocker or plop down on a crate to hear tales being told and talk about the weather. Feeling the breeze blowing off the water in the back door and drinking a soda from a glass bottle made one want to stay awhile. (Randy O'Neal.)

Showing off their hefty catches of speckled trout are, from left to right, Thomas "Tomboy" Baum, Randy O'Neal, Ginger Pledger, Walter Baum, and Mack Etheridge. The young men worked as mates on the boats. Pledger worked in the store and did not catch any fish that day but was pulled into the scene by the photographer who always wanted a pretty girl in the picture. (Aycock Brown Collection, Randy O'Neal.)

Bill Merritt (right) had been a director at an agricultural institute in Farmingdale, New York, before retiring to Wanchese. While fishing out of Mack's Fishing Center with mate Randy O'Neal (left) and Mack Etheridge (center) in April 1959, they landed 40 flounder and 10 bluefish. Everything was legal, and there were no limits. (Aycock Brown Collection, Randy O'Neal.)

"No Fish—No Pay," the motto associated with Mack's Fishing Center, was in bold print in this 1971 advertisement in the *Coastland Times*. Mack had Burma-Shave–style signs along the road from Nags Head to Wanchese advertising his business and always finishing with his motto. In later years, he increased his store inventory to sell marine supplies like propellers, pumps, and motors to commercial fishermen. (Randy O'Neal.)

Many local families made a living by accommodating fishermen. Vince and Erma Midgett owned the Cavalier Motor Court in Manns Harbor in the 1950s and 1960s. Out of a large frame house, they operated a grocery downstairs and a boardinghouse upstairs. There were three cabins behind that. Their son Lloyd Midgett was the guide and most likely took out this party who caught a load of striped bass. (OBHC.)

This family who worked at Pepsi-Cola came from Durham, North Carolina, to freshwater fish in South Lake, a remote body of water on the Dare County mainland. The swampy wilderness is also teaming with bear and deer, and regular clientele from the mountains of North Carolina and Virginia come to hunt with native guides who work in both the hunting and fishing trades. (Aycock Brown Collection, OBHC.)

A native of Long Island, New York, George Dykstra, posing with a sunfish, moved to the Outer Banks and opened Dyke's Fishing Center in the late 1930s on Roanoke Island near present-day Pirate's Cove Marina. The fishing center was formerly known as Rodger's Place. Dykstra's newly purchased home and store were on a small spit of land bordered by canals at the foot of the bridge to Nags Head. (Faye Dykstra Austin.)

As seen in this photograph, when the first wooden bridge to Nags Head was in place, the highway passed right in front of Dyke's Fishing Center. The party boats for hire were lined up against a bulkhead; a dock would come later. Owner George Dykstra booked fishing parties for captains docked there. Sambo Tillett also booked trips that left Dyke's from Sam and Omie's Restaurant in Nags Head. (Faye Dykstra Austin.)

An adventurous tourist could also rent a rowboat that was kept in the back canal at Dyke's Fishing Center. In the late 1930s and early 1940s, charter captains from Manteo and Wanchese moved their boats to Dyke's Fishing Center, where tourists could more easily find them. During this era, the Dyke's fleet started making its way farther and farther out into the ocean for game fish. (Faye Dykstra Austin.)

The concrete Washington Baum Bridge to Nags Head was completed in 1962, putting Dyke's Fishing Center on the south side of the road that ran to the span. Dan Lewark (second from right) and his brother Rondal Lewark (left) took out this party of victorious fishermen. At the end of the day, fish that already showed signs of wear were wrapped up in a canvas tarpaulin and put in the trunk of the car. (NPS, CHNS.)

Dan Lewark (left) and his brother Rondal (right) took special care of *Rita,* named for Dan's daughter. When hurricanes threatened, Dyke's Fishing Center captains moved their boats up the canal for protection, almost to the Manteo/Wanchese intersection. The Lewarks stayed aboard during a storm to loosen and tighten mooring lines as the tide fluctuated. Once during a hurricane, they rescued a stray dog paddling for its life. Dan took it home, and it became the family pet, Spot. (Faye Dykstra Austin.)

By suspending a signboard with a line, Ken Ward made sure his customer would remember with whom he caught this marlin in the mid-1950s. Members of the tight-knit Outer Banks community were well acquainted with every boat docked at Dyke's Fishing Center. They knew its builder, all the owners, and all the tales of all the fish that were caught from it. One local said, "Each boat had a personality." (Faye Dykstra Austin.)

Joe Berry of Manteo sat on the washboard of his commercial shad boat, *Ella View,* in Dykstra's Ditch. Berry was the only black captain in the charter fleet and was well respected by his peers. A few individuals who made reservations through Dyke's Fishing Center balked when they saw their captain and mate were black men. One fisherman asked Dan Lewark, who always berthed next to Berry, to take him out instead of Berry. Lewark, who did not have a charter that day, fired back a strong negative reply. (OBHC.)

It was getting dark by the time Joe Berry (second from left) and his party had their photograph taken by Dykstra's Ditch. Berry was such a gentleman that he always radioed other captains to tell them where fish were biting. One day, fellow charter captain Dan Lewark saw a water spout pick up Berry's boat, *Phyllis Mae,* spin it around, and set it back down. (Faye Dykstra Austin.)

On Dyke's Fishing Center dock, Dan Lewark (right) held in his left hand a white marlin that was probably hit by a shark. In the days before the catch-and-release mindset, every fish that was caught was brought back to shore. After a picture was snapped, fish that were not particularly good to eat were thrown overboard into the ditch for the crabs to do their work. (Faye Dykstra Austin.)

This fishing party who went out on the *Maggie* got their money's worth in dolphin on this day in 1947. In the 1950s, many captains moved their boats from Dyke's Fishing Center to Oregon Inlet Fishing Center. Oregon Inlet was more up-to-date and a few miles closer to the Gulf Stream, the new destination fishing grounds where many paying parties wanted to go. (Faye Dykstra Austin.)

Five

INTO THE GULF STREAM

When sport fishermen from the north made local captains aware of the fish that were within reach just offshore, the race to the Gulf Stream began. Willie Etheridge Jr. used World War II naval ocean charts to plot a course offshore. He caught the first marlin that was brought into Oregon Inlet Fishing Center in 1953. Moon Tillett (third from left) and his son Billy Carl had a photograph taken with the monumental fish. (Billy Carl Tillett.)

The Perry brothers from Kitty Hawk started keeping their charter boats in a small shallow cut near Oregon Inlet for quicker ocean access. When the National Park Service purchased the area, that cut was transformed into a small harbor to promote recreational fishing. This 1956 aerial shot of the north side of Oregon Inlet, before a bridge was built, showed the ferry dock on the left and a newly completed fishing center complex on the right. (NPS, CHNS.)

In July 1956, this 324-pound blue marlin was on display at Oregon Inlet Fishing Center. Captains were converting surplus World War II LORAN navigational systems that came out of airplanes for use on their charter boats. They also stayed in touch with each other using shortwave radios. As it was with their seafaring forefathers, they depended on the lighthouses, landmarks, and fixed sea buoys for orientation. (NPS, CHNS.)

Just as fishing piers were unique concessions built on park service land, so, too, was the Oregon Inlet Fishing Center. A 10-year concessioner's contract for the center was awarded to Toby Tillett in 1950. For the previous 25 years, Tillett had operated a ferry service between Bodie and Pea Islands, daily navigating unpredictable Oregon Inlet without ever losing a car. He sold his ferry business to the state. (NPS, CHNS.)

In the early 1950s, Toby Tillett (right) chats with his nephew Omie Tillett at a well-stocked tackle counter within Oregon Inlet Fishing Center. Toby's wife, Zeta, knew that Toby was used to being outside and his own boss in his independent ferry service. When she heard that Toby won the concessioner's contract, she said, "It will never last." (Aycock Brown Collection, Margaret Tillett Daniels.)

The first concession building at Oregon Inlet Fishing Center was located at the mouth of the creek on the eastern side of the boat slips. Before Toby Tillett had the contract, Zeke Midgett from neighboring Currituck County ran the concession. The signs on Toby's Place indicated that the center would be open early enough to provide breakfast for parties before they left the dock. (NPS, CHNS.)

Oregon Inlet Fishing Center improved under Toby Tillett's tenure. He widened the creek and built retaining walls like the one shown in the foreground of this March 1954 photograph. He removed the old concession building and replaced it with a different building on the north side of the marina at the head of the creek. In the early days, finger piers extended out into the water. (NPS, CHNS.)

A shark was hoisted up using a block and tackle rig at Oregon Inlet Fishing Center in 1955. There to catch all the action with a camera always in hand was photographer Aycock Brown (right). Brown was the first director of the tourist bureau in Manteo. He took his mission to make the Outer Banks known to the wider world seriously. Snapping pictures of happy anglers and their catches was his specialty. (NPS, CHNS.)

Charlie and Nettie Brown enjoyed a 7Up break with "Gan-Gan" (Aycock Brown) on a dock at Oregon Inlet Fishing Center in the early 1950s. Brown would take a picture of a fishing party and send the photograph to the angler's hometown newspaper. It gave the fisherman a thrill to see his face in print and relive the triumphant day. It also drew potential fishing tourists to the Outer Banks. (Nettie Brown Tisch.)

With the help of his young mate, Billy Daniels, Moon Tillett in his captain's hat helped his party bring in channel bass and small bluefish on this 1950 inshore fishing day. For the price of a few dollars, photographer Aycock Brown could send a copy of this picture that he developed himself to any of the party members. Brown made sure captains and mates got photographs, too. (Aycock Brown Collection, Billy Carl Tillett.)

Once a car pulled off the pavement, the possibility of getting stuck in the sand became a probability. In July 1957, service crews laid surplus rubber matting that would later be anchored in place to create parking spaces at Oregon Inlet Fishing Center. Tourists loved to wander about the marina, crabbing off the docks and waiting for the fleet to return with their fascinating catches. (NPS, CHNS.)

In 1960, an extended parking area was created for Oregon Inlet Fishing Center. Tourist bureau director Aycock Brown did a fantastic job of promoting the Outer Banks. He developed friendships with newspaper editors who would use his fishing photographs as fillers in their copy. A special bond with an editor in Pittsburgh may account for the large number of Pennsylvania tourists who bypassed other beaches to get to North Carolina. (NPS, CHNS.)

Cape Hatteras National Seashore planners located a campground on the ocean side across from Oregon Inlet Fishing Center so that tourists could stay right where they wanted to fish. Trailer camping was becoming popular with Americans who wanted to connect with nature while having modern conveniences. Many summer romances took place between visiting teenage girls and Oregon Inlet fleet teenage mates. (NPS, CHNS.)

Commercial fishing boats catching winter flounder along the beachfront were docked at Oregon Inlet Fishing Center in January 1955. When recreational charter fishing first began, captains took on the hard task of transforming their commercial fishing boats to sport fishing boats as the seasons changed. The renowned *Erma Queen*, which landed more than her share of billfish, was rigged up here with a flounder net for commercial fishing. (NPS, CHNS.)

As evidenced by these workboats in 1955, both commercial and sport fisheries were thriving, and many boat owners had to make a decision as to which way to permanently go. Switching fisheries was time-consuming and expensive, and the older boats were too slow for quick day trips. The competition was keen among captains to build a sleeker, faster sport fishing boat with up-to-date features like fighting chairs. (NPS, CHNS.)

Older gasoline engine boats took three hours to get to the Gulf Stream. To redeem the time, captains would set up their customers to "fast troll" on the way out by dragging artificial lures from rods. Oftentimes, a lot of fish would be caught before the boat ever got to prime fishing grounds. When Moon Tillett (right) faced the crossroads of investing in a better boat or getting out of sport fishing, he chose to enter into a full-time commercial operation. (Billy Carl Tillett.)

Willie Etheridge Jr.'s success as the first Oregon Inlet fleet captain to land a blue marlin was certainly not because he had the best boat and the best equipment. On the contrary, he relied on his own innovation, work ethic, and courage. With very little information on how to participate in a new type of fishery, Etheridge used his knowledge of fish behavior to formulate a plan to go after a blue marlin. (Willie Etheridge III.)

Surrounded by hooks and lures, Willie Etheridge Jr. concentrates on getting ready for the next day's fishing. Etheridge arrived at the same crossroads of picking full-time sport fishing or full-time commercial fishing that fellow Wancheser Moon Tillett did. Etheridge also chose commercial fishing. Both Tillett and Etheridge established fish companies that bought and sold millions of pounds of seafood over the years. (Willie Etheridge III.)

During the era of this September 1957 photograph, some captains transported ice to their boats and went freely at all hours into Dare County Ice and Cold Storage Company in Manteo. One late night an unthinking captain put a load of squid into a bin of crushed ice, then picked up the squid to use as bait for his charter early the next morning. An unsuspecting ice crew bagged that fishy ice as potable for deliveries to stores. Dare Ice owner Alvah Ward Jr. said the incident almost put him out of business. (NPS, CHNS.)

In 1957, Toby Tillett sold his Oregon Inlet Fishing Center concession contract to the Creef Wescott Corporation, a family group who held a variety of businesses, including movie theaters in Manteo and Elizabeth City, a Texaco dealership in Manteo, and horse breeding and racing farms in two counties. Herbert Augustus "H.A." Creef Jr. became the on-site manager at Oregon Inlet Fishing Center. This August 1958 photograph showed the addition of a restaurant on the west side of the building. (NPS, CHNS.)

In January 1962, Oregon Inlet Fishing Center was a quiet spot. H.A. Creef and staff prepared the marina for a busy charter season ahead. Little did they know that two months later, their hard work would be in shambles. With no warning, a late winter nor'easter, the Great Atlantic Coast Storm of 1962, hit the Outer Banks on March 7. Aycock Brown dubbed it the Ash Wednesday Storm. (NPS, CHNS.)

The Ash Wednesday Storm was classified as an extratropical cyclone. It occurred during a spring tide, the exact time when the sun, moon, and earth aligned to produce the highest tide. At Outer Banks Fishing Center, the old store was swept away, leaving the newer part that had been a restaurant. In spite of pounding waves, a mounted trophy fish still hung on the restaurant wall. (NPS, CHNS.)

During the Ash Wednesday Storm, gas pumps went in the creek, and underground tanks were compromised. Both cement and asphalt pavements broke up like peanut brittle as the sand was washed out from underneath. Wooden boats broke their ropes and rode the extremely high tide up onto the sand. Manager H.A. Creef said that a tidal wave from the ocean hit Oregon Inlet Fishing Center. (Creef family.)

A commercial fisherman attempted to wall off a workspace with plywood. He was trying to get a pump going to pull water out of his vessel and raise it up from the boat basin floor. The Ash Wednesday Storm produced dangerous conditions and record snowfalls all over the East Coast. No one was killed locally in the storm, but many residents experienced traumatic moments in which they thought they would die. (Creef family.)

This aerial photograph was taken as recovery from the Ash Wednesday Storm was underway, but the path that the ocean made to Oregon Inlet Fishing Center can still be traced on the upper left side. A dredge (on the right) began to dig out tons of sand from the boat basin. Many of the finger piers were destroyed in the storm, and the remaining ones would fall to the dredge. (Aycock Brown Collection, Creef family.)

Outer Banks natives were experts at getting back on their feet after a storm hit. Oregon Inlet Fishing Center was rebuilt quickly so that a season of fishing revenue would not be lost. The boat basin was dug out and rimmed with bulkheads and docks. The ferry (right) was loaded with Hatteras-bound cars, but it would soon be obsolete as the Herbert C. Bonner Bridge over Oregon Inlet was almost complete. (NPS, CHNS.)

A new concession building was constructed after the Ash Wednesday Storm of 1962. A short time later, it was moved to the west side of the marina. In front of the new building, Buddy Cannady (third from right) had a captain's raccoon eyes brought about by wearing sunglasses daily. He and his mate, Ralph Wayne Johnson (right), helped their party land dolphin, oceanic bonito, and even a sea turtle that was not protected by law during that era. (Doc Davis photograph; Creef family.)

H.A. Creef's wife, Liz (left), and blonde five-year-old daughter Liz Ann pose with a marlin in 1963. H.A. Creef found it challenging to run the fishing center under the vigilant superintendency of the National Park Service. After being told the spikes on the fish display board were hazardous to bystanders, Creef invented a system that retracted the boards when no fish were on them. (Creef family.)

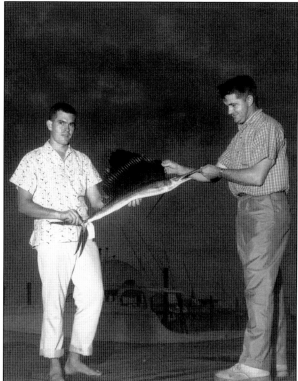

In the early 1960s, H.A. Creef (right) holds a juvenile sailfish with Jackie Cox, who had just come home from the Korean War and was working as a dockhand. Creef's family corporation held the concession contract on Oregon Inlet Fishing Center until about 1965. They sold the contract, in part because they had just opened Duke of Dare Motor Lodge in Manteo. Dick O'Neal of New Holland, a small town in nearby Hyde County, bought the contract. (Creef family.)

When the concession contract once again became available for Oregon Inlet Fishing Center, a group of charter captains retained a lawyer and formed a corporation, the Oregon Inlet Guides Association. They won the contract and held it through 2017. On March 15, 1967, at a meeting held in the Dare County Courthouse, Chick Craddock presided from the judge's bench and Harry Baum acted as secretary. (Aycock Brown Collection, OBHC.)

Members of the Oregon Inlet Guides Association sat in the courtroom gallery during a nighttime meeting on March 15, 1967. From left to right are (first row) Tony Tillett, Jesse Etheridge, Joe Berry, Warren Gallop, Buddy Cannady, and Charles Midgett; (second row) Warren O'Neal and Wayland Baum; (third row) Omie Tillett, possibly Dick O'Neal, and Marvin Mann. (Aycock Brown Collection, OBHC.)

In rough seas on August 11, 1966, two blue marlins were on two different lines at the same time from the *Mar-T-Moe*. Capt. Murray Cudworth (left) laid a knife on the fish box and told mate Billy Carl Tillett (second from right) to cut one of the lines if they tangled. Incredibly, they managed to land both fish. Cudworth saw a third marlin swimming nearby and told Tillett to put bait out. The exhausted client begged for mercy. (Billy Carl Tillett.)

Mate Billy Carl Tillett (left) helped this angler hold a sailfish that was caught aboard the round-stern *Slow an Easy*. Owner Fred Basnight and a group of Oregon Inlet captains went to Ocean City, Maryland, to learn more about bill fishing from highly experienced sport fishing captains. The first thing they found out was that their reels were not big enough. They brought back more findings to share with the whole fleet. (Billy Carl Tillett.)

The first sport fishing charter boats, like the *Tony*, had gasoline marine engines with every brand name, just like those on the open road. Each captain had his preference whether it was Lincoln, Ford, Chrysler, or Oldsmobile. In the late 1950s, gas-guzzling motors were replaced with more economical, military surplus diesel engines; however, the large diesels would not fit in some of the narrow, smaller boats. (Creef family.)

Early captains used onshore landmarks to navigate. Once when Harry Baum (right) was coming in from the Gulf Stream to Oregon Inlet, he saw the Wright Memorial in Kill Devil Hills and knew he was off course. He was operating an unfamiliar boat with no radio, and then he ran out of gas. The wind pushed his boat near a shoal, so he anchored, put on a life jacket, and swam for shore, leaving the party of six onboard. He found help at the Old Nags Head Coast Guard Station. (Creef family.)

One of the surprise bonuses of fishing offshore was catching tuna, a new fishery in its own right. Tuna were exhilarating to catch, especially using the primitive gear of the day. Local people had never eaten big game fish like tuna and dolphin before. When fishermen from other areas introduced them to the delicacy, they could not believe what they had been missing. (Creef family.)

When it was time to hoist the 805-pound tiger shark up on the dock, it was truly an all-hands-on-deck situation. Murray Cudworth in a khaki uniform pulled on the tail rope. Also in khakis, Billy Brown had the middle rope. Tony Tillett was shirtless, and Richard Baum was the last man on the right. If a fisherman caught a shark and wanted to bring it to the dock, it would be dragged behind the boat. (Creef family.)

Hundreds of tourists came to Oregon Inlet Fishing Center every afternoon when the boats returned from offshore fishing. Onlookers waited in anticipation while the boats slowly backed into their slips. With dramatic flair, the mates tossed dolphins and tuna up on the dock for up-close examination. When a big marlin was brought in, it was theater at its greatest. (Lois Midgett Dunnigan.)

Families of the captains and their mates spent many hours at Oregon Inlet Fishing Center often waiting for their relatives to come in. Children played on the docks and caught crabs with a line baited with a chicken neck. The Brown children, from left to right, Mike, Cindy, Nettie, and Margaret, are waiting for their father, Brantley, or their uncle Billy. Their grandfather Aycock took their picture. (Nettie Brown Tisch.)

Six

BROTHERS AT SEA

Three of the finest fishermen the Outer Banks has ever produced pose with 40 channel bass caught in just an hour and a half. Omie Tillett (second from left), Moon Tillett (third from left), and Willie Etheridge Jr. (right) kept a pure love of fishing, untainted by the day-in, day-out grind of the sport fishing industry. The fisherman on the far left died shortly after this day, and the story circulated that the big three killed a man by fishing him to death. (Billy Carl Tillett.)

Tony Tillett (right) showed more enthusiasm than his father, Sam "Sambo" Tillett (left), at the catch of a blue and a white marlin at Oregon Inlet Fishing Center in the late 1950s. Sambo, as well as his brothers, cousins, and sons Omie and Tony, were pioneers in offshore fishing. Their expertise gave birth to the saying, "If you're not fishing with a Tillett, you're not fishing." (Tony Tillett.)

Tony Tillett (left) did not have to rely on his movie-star good looks to win over customers. His parties consistently caught fish aboard the Carolinian, the name that he has given to five boats over 60 years. He did a stint as a boatbuilder when he and his brother Omie built his second Carolinian together at Omie's Sportsman Boatworks on Roanoke Island. (d'Amours Studio photograph; Creef family.)

Tony Tillett sits at the feet of his older brother Omie (center). Tony Tillett has taken more people fishing than can be counted. At age 82, he received the Tommy Gifford Award from the International Game Fish Association in Dania Beach, Florida. He limits his fishing to inshore now, getting a chuckle when his longtime customers call to book a trip saying, "Are you still alive?" (Tony Tillett.)

On May 9, 1965, Chester Tillett (second from right) and mate Billy Carl Tillett (right) put their anglers on a load of channel bass from aboard the *Tony*. It was not always easy to work with family. Chester's son Kirby recalled one day while working as a mate for his father, he missed gaffing a fish. His dad cursed and embarrassed him over the miss, and right there at the green buoy 30 miles offshore, Kirby quit his job. (Billy Carl Tillett.)

Celebrating a huge catch of channel bass are locals, from left to right, (first row) Capt. Omie Tillett, Jule Burris, and Guy Midgett; (second row) Janie Etheridge Ernst, Camille Midgett Podolski, and Jean Parker. A captain had to be a jack-of-all-trades, fixing mechanical breakdowns at sea. Omie Tillett was the man on the water to call for help. If all efforts failed to restore power, any of the fleet captains would give a tow back to the dock. (Aycock Brown Collection, OBHC.)

Sport fishing is often intertwined with the hard-partying world. An exception was Omie Tillett, captain of the *Sportsman*. He had a conversion experience and became a deeply committed Christian. He made numerous disciples for Jesus among the Oregon Inlet fleet family by showing true faith with his words and actions. Each morning over the radio, he would pray for God's protection and blessings as the boats headed to the Gulf Stream. (Lois Midgett Dunnigan.)

In 1988, Omie Tillett spreads a coat of varnish on the teak trim of his sport fishing boat, the *Sportsman*, when a nor'easter kept him at the dock. Many of the men who worked as a mate for Tillett went on to own and run their own boats. Respect for "Captain Omie" ran so deeply that several children have been named for him, including his great-granddaughter Omie Gornell. (Drew Wilson Collection, OBHC.)

John Bayliss of the *Tarheel* checks the weight of a tuna in 1980, his first year as a captain at Oregon Inlet. Prior to that, he worked as a mate in Hatteras on *Early Bird*, in Florida on *Temptress*, and at Oregon Inlet on *Fight-N-Lady*. Like Omie Tillett, he became a boatbuilder when he built his own sportfisher and other captains put in an order. Bayliss always asked Tillett to pray when a completed sport fishing yacht was christened at Bayliss Boatworks. (Drew Wilson Collection, OBHC.)

Wayland Baum (right) liked to solve his own problems; although, he once called for Coast Guard assistance when an oil hose burst while he was running the *Mel-O-Dee*. The inexperienced Coast Guard crew threw him a line and then backed over their tow hawser and wrapped it around their propeller. Baum told them to forget it and called his son Billy for a tow instead. (Creef family.)

With fish slung over his back, Billy Baum struck a pose for the photographer similar to a pose his father, Wayland Baum, had struck decades before with decoys. Confident and capable, Billy brought in the fish on *Kay* and later on *Dream Girl*. He also had natural talent as a boatbuilder and could draw the water line freehand by the rock of the eye on an unpainted hull. (Aycock Brown Collection, OBHC.)

On July 26, 1974, Harry Baum noticed a big swirl under a ballyhoo bait being dragged from an outrigger. When he made a circle to check it out, he saw a huge blue marlin with a bill that looked like a baseball bat shoving up a one-foot-high sea. In a short time, fisherman Jack Herrington was hooked up and began a battle that would last two hours and 45 minutes. The fish was so large that it could not jump and perform its beautiful dance upon the water. Mate Richard Baum gaffed the exhausted giant and held it with two hand gaffs. Captain Harry radioed a nearby boat for help in getting the beast aboard. The low gunnels of the *Jo-Boy, the* smallest boat in the Oregon Inlet fleet, worked to the gang's advantage as they heaved the wide fish over and in. The captain suspected that the marlin could be a world record and let it be known what he potentially had. He was so keyed up and nervous that he almost ran into the dock that he had backed up to hundreds of times. The scales at Oregon Inlet Fishing Center only went to 1,000 pounds, so the marlin was loaded into Buddy Davis's pickup and taken down to the Hatteras Marlin Club to be weighed. A caravan of excited onlookers followed the truck. The marlin probably lost 10 percent of its weight in its travels, but it still tipped the scales at 1,142 pounds, enough to certify it as a world record that would stand for 11 years. A shocked Harry (center) is photographed with his sons Junior (left) and Jerald (right). Junior usually worked as Harry's mate but happened to be off that day. He made it to Hatteras for the picture. (Joanne Baum Clift.)

Bobby Scarborough (squatting on left) took lessons he learned from Willie Etheridge Jr. (squatting on right) to heart. He ran the *Red Fin* out of Oden's Dock at Hatteras and was known as an enthusiastic captain who would go out no matter what the weather. Etheridge had the same drive. Once a pilot pointed out a school of red drum from the air to Etheridge, his passenger. The pilot later said, "Captain Will caught everyone of them throughout the summer." (Willie Etheridge III.)

This party caught these tuna with Charles Midgett (left) on the *Lois C* by trolling ballyhoo beneath the water's surface. Midgett later brought a new technology he had seen in Hawaii to the fleet. The green stick, a 34-to-45-foot-long flexible fiberglass pole mounted to the deck, causes plastic squid lures to skip along the surface. Midgett experimented while other captains laughed—until they saw his results. (Lois Midgett Dunnigan.)

Mate Balfour Baum (left) and Capt. Charles Midgett (second from left) were happy for a teenage Garry Oliver, who scored a blue marlin in 1964. Five years later at age 23, Oliver bought a pier in South Nags Head and named it the Outer Banks Fishing Pier. Fishing has been Oliver's lifelong vocation and passion. He also owns a tackle shop and boat rental business, Fishing Unlimited, on the Nags Head causeway. (M.D. "Doc" Davis photograph; Lois Midgett Dunnigan.)

Murray Cudworth (kneeling on right) had saltwater in his veins. He was always the final captain back to the dock, hating to give up until the last fish was caught. He had the skills but not the equipment, so when his slow boat could no longer compete, he managed Oregon Inlet Fishing Center for the Oregon Inlet Guides Association for four years. He soon got back on the water running a private boat, the *Fish-N-Fool*. (Billy Carl Tillett.)

On this day in May 1965, Jesse Etheridge's boat brought 581 bluefish to Oregon Inlet Fishing Center. These tough guy fishermen with their fedoras and wristwatches were at the other end of the cultural spectrum from their captain. Most assuredly, Etheridge used his wide-open personality to find common ground with them. Since Etheridge was colorblind, his *Caredwyn* was a patchwork of many colors. (Robin Daniels Holt.)

Kitty Hawker Lee Perry (center) spoke with a lisp, and sometimes his parties confessed that they did not understand a word he said. Perry snacked on soda crackers during his days on the *Deepwater*. When a big fish was hooked, he would yell and spit crackers everywhere in his excitement. "Soda crackers all over the bridge" has become a phrase used within the fishing world to synonymously explain the thrill of blue marlin action. (Creef family.)

Rudolph Peele included his daughter in this shot with a large dolphin. He named his first boat for her, building the 54-foot-long *Martha Ann* in the backyard of his grandfather Irving Stowe's home in Manteo. Despite working long hours, Peele was an involved father, getting home in time to watch his son Wesley so his wife and daughter could play colonist roles in *The Lost Colony*, the nighttime outdoor drama. (Maxine Peele.)

The men who formed the Oregon Inlet Guides Association were a tight-knit brotherhood. Some members took their mutual business dealings a step further by forming another corporation and buying a bottom-fishing headboat together. Wesley "Rudolph" Peele was one of the original stockholders in the boat that would eventually be named the *Miss Oregon Inlet*. (Maxine Peele.)

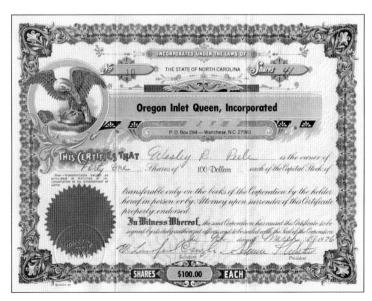

At age 15, Ben Midgett (left) received the Carnegie Medal, the highest honor for civilian heroism, for rescuing two boys from drowning in the summer of 1960. Pres. Dwight D. Eisenhower presented a bronze medal and a $500 award to Midgett in a ceremony at the White House. The official account of the day stated that Midgett was working as a mate for Willie Etheridge Sr. (right) on the *Boys* when they saw a family in a motorboat capsize in Oregon Inlet. The occupants were trapped beneath the overturned boat except for eight-year-old David Batten, who had been thrown clear. Captain Etheridge took his boat as close as he could in the four-foot breakers, and Midgett jumped in fully clothed and barefoot. He swam 40 yards to David and towed him back to the charter boat. After rescuing the first boy, Midgett went back to the disabled craft. He swam another 60 feet through the breakers and took William Batten, age 11, from the arms of a man who was struggling to keep him above water. Midgett was getting tired but managed to make progress. A rope was thrown from the *Boys*, Midgett grabbed it, and both he and William were pulled in and lifted aboard. Other parties rescued the adults, but a four-year-old drowned that day. As an adult, Midgett never mentioned the incident, even to close friends. (Aycock Brown Collection, Tracy Midgett Leonard.)

While steering northwest to come back to Oregon Inlet from the Gulf Stream on the *Mighty Wind*, Warren Gallop (at the wheel) had the overwhelming urge to turn west. He traveled three and a half miles off course, and just when he muttered, "This is foolish," he saw two exhausted men hanging onto a flimsy rubber raft that had been pulled out to sea. He never learned the names of the ones he rescued but said, "The Spirit of the Lord led me." (Margie Gallop Tillett.)

After 22 years in the Coast Guard, Marvin Mann (left) got his dream job as a captain, taking parties like these anglers into the sound for striped bass. He bought a Harkers Island boat for ocean fishing and named it the *Playboy*, a name his wife was not happy about. His customers included singer Jimmy Fortune of the Statler Brothers and actor Andy Griffith. Even though he was tight with a dollar, he hung on to Griffith's check for a long time to cherish the signature. (Billy Carl Tillett.)

When Billy Brown (right) returned from the Vietnam War, he taught history in Manteo schools and ran charters on the *Erma Queen*. For decades, he gathered enough fishing stories each summer to keep his students entertained the whole school year. With the boat's reputation for raising fish and Brown's skill in finding them, they had a stellar run before they both retired at the same time. (Aycock Brown Collection, OBHC.)

"Sweet William" Smith moved to the Outer Banks for peace and quiet. He was traumatized by an event that occurred on a bus overtaken by rioting convicts while he was a prison guard. In 1973, he got a job as a mate on *Stormy Duchess* with Lunsford Crew, who also hailed from Roanoke Rapids. Crew, who came from a wealthy family, was accepted by the captains who came up the hard way. (Allison Smith Lopez.)

SKIPPER

While fishing on the *Skipper* with Buddy Davis (right), a rod snapped and mate Dean Johnson (left) quickly grabbed the line and brought up the expensive reel. He took it a step further when he hand-lined up this white marlin. In the winter, Johnson worked in Florida, where he fine-tuned his fishing skills. He said, "Fishing on the Outer Banks was too easy, so easy that you didn't get a chance to improve." (Dean Johnson.)

Allan Foreman (left) and Dean Johnson (right) took second place in the first annual Oregon Inlet Billfishing Tournament in 1976. They were two out of a team of six who fished on Foreman's *Gal-O-Mine*. In the late 1970s, Foreman would be one of the first captains to move his boat to Pirate's Cove Marina in Manteo, a project that he developed. Johnson would graduate from mate and become captain of many boats that he built himself. (Dean Johnson.)

July 3, 1973, was a big day for Oregon Inlet Fishing Center customers. The captains and mates got a chance to pose, too. They are, from left to right, Bull Tolson, Mike Bennett, Buddy Davis, Dean Johnson, Billy Brown, Tommy Peters (kneeling), Billy Holton, Paul Spencer, Harry "Junior" Baum, and Harry Baum Sr. Johnson said, "In the early days, the mindset was kill, kill, kill. There was peer pressure and competition. Now, I just enjoy nature." (Dean Johnson.)

Charles Perry (left) and Tony Tillett (right) shared some evening downtime. Perry has fished off Australia, Africa, and Costa Rica, although he prefers the home waters of the Gulf Stream. He has the reputation of being the world's best heavy tackle wireman. When the angler has finished his reeling, the wireman takes over by grabbing the leader and using his skill and strength to bring the fish in close enough to be tagged and measured before release. (Tony Tillett.)

Mitchell Bateman (left) was once dragged underwater by a blue marlin after Bateman grabbed the leader and wrapped the wire in his hand. The marlin dove under the boat, shot up at the stern, and popped Bateman up and overboard. As he was pulled deeper by the plunging fish, it took Bateman a moment to unclench the wire and free himself. By that time, because he was so deep in the water, the boat above him appeared to be just a few inches long. (Mitchell Bateman.)

The local notion that boatbuilding is an inherent skill proved to be true in the life of Buddy Davis, who descended from a long line of boat craftsmen. Although he spent many years as a charter captain, his true calling was realized when he started building sportfishers in the Carolina flare style. Davis was the first to make fiberglass-molded boats in a production facility on Roanoke Island. (Drew Wilson Collection, OBHC.)

Wearing his customer's hat, Buddy Cannady (third from left) ended another fine day of fishing by cozying up to this lady angler and her Yorkshire terrier. Cannady built a new boat in a barn in his yard every winter, ran it as a charter sportfisher in the summer, and sold it in the fall. It seemed like each one of them were named the *Capt. BC.* The boats built at lightning speed were starkly simple and known to raise fish. (Creef family.)

Arvin Midgett (right) was one of the original stockholders in the Oregon Inlet Guides Association who leased Oregon Inlet Fishing Center from the National Park Service. That contract lasted over 50 years, and descendants of those original stockholders received dividends up until the contract ended at the end of 2017. When Midgett was not aboard his *Miss Boo II*, he was building skiffs between 16 and 25 feet long for duck hunting and shallow-water fishing. (Dean Johnson.)

Mike Hayman worked hard to make the Seafare into an elegant Nags Head restaurant with quality food and impeccable service by waiters in short red coats and bow ties. Attending a fishing tournament banquet in their own restaurant in the late 1970s was the Hayman family. From left to right are Shaun, Mike, Rachel, and Todd. Todd Hayman is sitting on the lap of Rachel's uncle Rudolph Peele, who attended with them. (Aycock Brown Collection, Maxine Peele.)

The Seafare restaurant was doing a booming business, and the Haymans lived a life that reflected that. Mike Hayman was one of the first locals to buy a pleasure yacht. He named the well-appointed craft *My Lady Rachel* and hired Rudolph Peele (standing on right) to be captain. High-rolling Mike (left) and gorgeous Rachel (kneeling on left) were the golden couple until Rachel passed away from breast cancer in 1978. (Maxine Peele.)

Way ahead of his time, Oregon Inlet Fishing Center restaurant manager Gene Prieser struck a deal with Mike Hayman to rent *My Lady Rachel* for $125 for his daughter's wedding in 1977. Hayman stipulated no shoes on the boat, except for grandparents. The wedding party had to wait until all the charter boats finished fueling up so that Rudolph Peele could back the large yacht up to the dock. (Pixie Prieser Wescott.)

The idea was to get married at sea, but the officiant, Bill Anderson of the Barefoot Trader Store in Kitty Hawk, revealed at the last minute that he was susceptible to seasickness. Tommy and Pixie Wescott were married on the flying bridge while their guests stood on the dock. The mother of the bride, Pat Prieser, said, "I can't hear, and I'm paying for this." The wedding party took a short cruise afterward. (Pixie Prieser Wescott.)

Seven

HATTERAS CLOUT

In the early 1950s, Brenda Styron touched the dorsal fin of a blue marlin caught on her father's boat out of Hatteras. Lashed by their tails to a pump pipe, two marlins were pulled up together by a single block and tackle. The primitive harbor, like Oregon Inlet Fishing Center's harbor, was initially very shallow but was dredged out to make it deeper at a time before governmental agencies had oversight. (Little Edgar Styron.)

In the 1930s, when most of his peers were commercial fishing, Ernal Foster sought to develop a charter sport fishing industry on Hatteras Island. Putting his finances and reputation at risk in 1937, Foster supplied the white cedar to have a classic Core Sound round-stern boat built for $805 in Marshallberg, North Carolina. Foster thought the *Albatross* was perfectly suited for taking parties to the ocean for $25 or inshore for $15. During this era, avid sportsmen from Maryland and New Jersey were making their way to Hatteras, knowing it was in close proximity to the Gulf Stream. These fishermen enlightened the locals about the amazing game fish that were just offshore. They often brought their own boats with outriggers, which caused speculation among the local men. After much trial and error, in 1938 Hugo Rutherford of Allamuchy, New Jersey, succeeded in catching a blue marlin from his boat *Mako*. Rutherford became friends with Foster and showed him what types of rods, reels, lines, and bait to use when going after blue marlin. Rutherford gave Foster his own set of outriggers, and after he acquired stronger tackle, Foster began regularly landing billfish, as seen in this 1940s photograph. (D. Victor Meekins Papers, OBHC.)

Offshore fishing came to a stop during World War II. After Ernal Foster returned from patrol duty, he added two more boats to his fleet. The first woman in North Carolina to catch a blue marlin was aboard the *Albatross II*. Betsy Walker of Richmond, Virginia, won the honor on July 13, 1951. Sharing the moment are, from left to right, Betsy Walker, Ross Walker, Ernal Foster, and mate Milton Meekins. (Aycock Brown Collection, OBHC.)

In the early 1990s, Ernal Foster sat with the *Albatross* fleet that has continuously given fishermen thrills and fish since 1937. The Fosters like to recall that when Ernal's dream to build an ocean sportfisher was ridiculed by fellow commercial fishermen and by potential boatbuilders, he said, "It's my wood and my money and if it does not turn out right, it is my problem." (Drew Wilson Collection, OBHC.)

Descending from generations of watermen, Edgar Styron was game to try anything new. In the early days, he and his wife let Ernal Foster keep the *Albatross* at their dock. They knew Foster's phone was ringing off the hook with charter inquiries. Styron's regular fishing customer, Walter Wilkins of Norfolk, cosigned a banknote for Styron so that he could also fully enter the race to the Gulf Stream. (*Salt Water Fisherman* photograph; Little Edgar Styron.)

With Gulf Stream fishing on his mind, Edgar Styron had *Twins* built on Harkers Island. It had two Chrysler Crown gasoline engines, and it was the first square-stern boat on Hatteras. Styron maneuvered *Twins* so adeptly that he caused his anglers to catch their marlins quickly. Other captains would let the customer fight for hours. The Hatteras fleet brought in two or three marlins every day. (Little Edgar Styron.)

The first blue marlin was brought to the Styron family dock in May 1953. Posing with the trophy are, from left to right, Little Edgar and Cathleen Styron, Florence and Harvey Young, and a tired-looking Edgar Styron. After the war, customers could take a trip to the Gulf Stream with Styron on the *Twins* for $65, fish in the inlet for $40, and get their catch cleaned for 3¢ a pound. (Little Edgar Styron.)

As the mother of five girls and two boys, Cathleen Stowe Styron somehow made time to work with her husband, Edgar Styron, in the family charter business and restaurant. On the day their restaurant opened in 1954, Cathleen went into labor and gave birth to baby Sue. Pictured here in the early 1950s are, from left to right, Little Edgar, Brenda, Sherry, Anne, and Cathleen Styron. (Little Edgar Styron.)

With financial backing from Norfolk, Edgar and Cathleen Styron built the Hatteras Marlin Restaurant, which opened for business in 1954. Cathleen handled the day-to-day operations at the restaurant while Edgar took out charter parties. They sold the restaurant in 1959, and it became a private clubhouse for the Hatteras Marlin Club. (Little Edgar Styron.)

These buddies are tickled with their big score of dolphin caught on the *Twins* with Edgar Styron (second from left). In the background to the right is the Hatteras Marlin Restaurant. The Styron family home is to the left. Techniques used to catch species that Hatteras men had not fished for before were often learned from visiting anglers. Local captains still had to find the fish by predicting where they would be and when they would show up. (Little Edgar Styron.)

Many successful businessmen like to come to Hatteras and enjoy good fishing and easy friendships with locals. Alexander Paul Kotarides of Norfolk, Virginia, was one such man. As a third-generation baker, he took Mary Jane Bakery from a local business to a large independent bakery that employed 450 people. He boosted his brand image with a cute little girl, a bright yellow plastic bag, and television advertisement. (Little Edgar Styron.)

Two children of Edgar Styron, twins Little Edgar and Sherry Lynn Styron born in 1951, were the inspiration to name his boat *Twins*. The best of pals, they shared red hair and spirited temperaments. Their father expanded his business when he had another square-stern Harkers Island boat built, *Twins II*, the first boat on Hatteras with a diesel engine and a flying bridge. (Little Edgar Styron.)

During this 1950s era, marlins were brought in, weighed, and then dumped at sea the following morning on the way to fish again. If the fish was going to be mounted as a trophy, the mate tagged it and stowed it in a walk-in freezer to be picked up later by a taxidermy company. At the end of the season, mates often received sizable commission checks from the taxidermist. (Little Edgar Styron.)

As an eight-year-old, Little Edgar Styron showed the adults how it was done by using his father's bamboo pole and leaning back on a unique fighting chair aboard *Twins I.* Little Edgar Styron's mother, Cathleen, wrote to sportswriters at the *Washington Post* to promote Hatteras fishing, telling them the tuna were stacked up like cordwood. She offered them a free trip offshore, and they took her up on it. (Little Edgar Styron.)

Little Edgar Styron's expression exudes pride and confidence after catching two bluefish. *Twins I* and *II* served the Styron family well. Years later, *Twins I* was named the *Duke of Dare* by another owner, and the Styrons grieved when they heard that it sank. Sometime later, a commercial fisherman pulled up part of the cabin in his net and knew instantly that it was *Twins I* by the porthole. He made it into a wall hanging. (Little Edgar Styron.)

In 1957, Nelson "Clam" Stowe ran charters for Edgar Styron. Stowe used crutches because of a permanent leg injury incurred when he was shot in midair as a World War II paratrooper. Writer Tom Jackson described Stowe as having "calloused hands that could handle a rope in heavy weather and yet were sensitive enough to feel the slightest nudge of a curious sheepshead against a piece of bait on a light line." (Little Edgar Styron.)

In the late 1970s, Spurgeon Stowe (in stripes) admired the marlin held by mate Mitchell Bateman (left) and caught on Ricky and Sue Haycox's the *Morning Star*. Stowe followed in the footsteps of his father, Clam, and took it to the next level by captaining a private boat. As part of the tradition, Sue Haycox got "creeked," or was thrown overboard, to celebrate her first marlin. Since she was a female boat owner, she was thrown into a swimming pool rather than the creek. (Mitchell Bateman.)

Ashton Styron of Harkers Island worked for a private boat owner, Walter Wilkins, on the *Jon Lee II* in Hatteras. A steady salary and having a relationship with the owner were upsides in captaining a private boat, however, having to go wherever and whenever the owner said was hard on a skipper's family life. Private mates had greater responsibility than charter mates with added days of preparing tackle and cleaning the boat. (Little Edgar Styron.)

Many dignitaries fished out of Hatteras. On June 7, 1958, Raleigh men Thad Eure (left), North Carolina secretary of state, and Carl Goersch (center), publisher of *The State* magazine, joined Walter Wilkins (right), a Norfolk automotive dealer, on the *Jon Lee II* for a triple-header day. Rather than keeping the paradise for themselves, these men in positions of influence helped to make the area known and accessible. (Little Edgar Styron.)

Native Lucy Allen Stowe was a woman who enjoyed fishing, especially with Edgar Styron on one of the *Twins*. She studied meteorology and atmospheric physics at the College of Charleston in South Carolina and became the head meteorologist at the Hatteras Weather Bureau Station. Another aspect of her respectability was that she smoked a pipe. (Little Edgar Styron.)

Sally Austin looked as if she were headed straight to her kitchen to fry up what she just caught. Hatteras Island residents of her generation experienced huge changes. Ernal Foster said in 1982, "The bridge ruined Hatteras—at least for us. Now we have to lock our doors, lock up the tackle on our boats, and take the keys out of cars. Would you believe someone stole an automobile here the other day?" (D. Victor Meekins Papers, OBHC.)

Even though he was a pioneer captain searching for blue marlin in the Gulf Stream, Edgar Styron actually preferred channel bass fishing close to home with a group of locals. Kicking off the 1961 season on March 12 with the first reported landed channel bass are, from left to right, Lee Peele, "Skeeter" Skiles (a highway patrolman stationed on Hatteras Island), Edgar Styron, Don Oden, and Nacy Midgette. (Little Edgar Styron.)

Edgar O. Hooper (left) and Rany B. Jennette (right) dominated the competition in the Nags Head Surf Fishing Tournament. They brought the action down the banks when both men helped to found the Cape Hatteras Anglers Club in 1957. Tournaments have been sponsored by the club ever since. The angler who catches the largest fish in the surf will have his name engraved on a plaque bearing Hooper's name. (D. Victor Meekins Papers, OBHC.)

On the second day of competition, Friday, November 4, 1988, more than 100 teams representing at least eight states participated in the 31st annual Cape Hatteras Anglers Club Surf Fishing Tournament. The crowd went down to the sea in boots at Cape Point with an incredible backdrop of the Cape Hatteras Lighthouse before it was moved 2,900 feet inland to a safer location in 1999. (Drew Wilson Collection, OBHC.)

Bluefish, flounder, and sea mullet were not going anywhere under the watchful eye of tournament chairman Ray Couch. The fish were caught during one session of the 31st Cape Hatteras Anglers Club Surf Fishing Tournament in 1988. Couch moved his family to Buxton in 1964 after retiring as an officer in the US Army. He was the owner of the Red Drum Shopping Center. (Drew Wilson Collection, OBHC.)

The anglers aboard Tex Ballance's *Escape II* were making catching marlin look easy. People from all over the fishing world were learning about what was being caught in Hatteras. After several years of friendly banter, a formal competition was arranged in 1961 between the Hatteras Marlin Club and the Marlin Club of Puerto Rico. Hatteras landed more fish and proudly won the title of "Billfish Capital of the World." (D. Victor Meekins Papers, OBHC.)

Just a portion of what was caught, eight huge marlins hang from a newly built structure at the conclusion of a new kind of island competition, the International Blue Marlin Tournament at Hatteras in June 1963. Poli Sheahan of Bethesda, Maryland, won first place with 1,725 points from four blue marlins. He planned on returning the next year to defend his title. (D. Victor Meekins Papers, OBHC.)

Hatteras waterfront buildings and property changed hands many times over the decades. In the early 1990s, Frank and Joan Nelms of Driver, Virginia, expected to sell the 98-slip Hatteras Marina for a price in excess of $2 million. Old-timers remembered when the O'Neal, Robinson, Oden, Ballance, Willis, Styron, Peele, and Foster families rented or owned the waterfront. (Drew Wilson Collection, OBHC.)

The owner of the famed *Jersey Devil* hired Little Edgar Styron to take a party to the Gulf Stream. They brought in this marlin with a girth of 100 inches and an estimated weight of over 1,300 pounds. The scale at the Hatteras docks got to 1,128 and stopped. The fish was so heavy that it tore in two. When hunting a blue marlin, a captain will seek "a pretty piece of water," something different in terms of depth, temperature, or a botanical feature that may attract a curious marlin. (Little Edgar Styron.)

Ugliest Shark This Season

THIS THRESHER SHARK weighing 417 pounds was caught by Edgar Styron of Hatteras (left) who was fishing aboard the private boat "Marlin." Shown with Styron are Mary Barnett and Oscar Amoroso from Atlantic Beach, N. Y. (Jane Oden photo, DCTB)

In the days after the hit movie *Jaws*, Little Edgar Styron hammed it up in front of the camera by posing with his face right by this thresher shark's head. A man on the dock thought the shark was still alive and plunged his knife into it to prove his point. It was. Then the knife-wielding man cut open the shark's belly and found three live shark pups. Styron let them go in the creek. (Little Edgar Styron.)

Eight

ENDLESS VARIETY

All fishermen believe that every day is an adventure as they see the wonders of creation and experience unlimited surprises. Watching the swift makeup of a storm and laying eyes on a waterspout like this one near Oregon Inlet Fishing Center may be a little more adventure than an angler is seeking, but, nonetheless, it is a thrill to witness the power of nature. (Brian Horsley.)

Pirates Cove on Roanoke Island began to take shape in the late 1970s. The densely developed, upscale housing community and marina featured dock space for property owners. To generate interest in the new marina, manager Jimmy Byrd persuaded Little Edgar Styron (without a shirt) to bring *Heritage Venture* there for a summer season. Styron brought game fish daily to a dock that did not have fish-cleaning facilities, scales, or a freezer. (Little Edgar Styron.)

Another captain at Pirates Cove in the early 1980s was Jimmy Feinman on the *Outlaw*. He remembered, "Everyone at Oregon Inlet thought we were fools." To draw in customers, he would nail the day's catch to a board by the highway to be seen by potential customers who were waiting for the drawbridge to close. Feinman, who would become a lawyer, once negotiated with a fisherman that if he did not get a marlin, he would only pay for gas. The fisherman paid for the full trip. (Drew Wilson Collection, OBHC.)

In 1980, the Oregon Inlet Fishing Center docking area was modernized by the installation of power and water lines to each slip. According to the National Park Service agreement, concessionaires are responsible for improvements and maintenance of the property. The concessionaire during the era of this photograph was the Oregon Inlet Guides Association. (NPS, CHNS.)

A new boardwalk completed the Oregon Inlet Fishing Center update in 1980. In 2018, brothers Russ and Stephen King and sister Kristen Robinson obtained a 20-year concession license for the fishing center. They are constructing an 11,000-square-foot, two-storied building at the north end of the basin to house a restaurant, ship's store, and museum. There will also be new fish-cleaning and freezing facilities and a pavilion for events like weddings and tournament celebrations. (NPS, CHNS.)

Mill Landing Harbor in Wanchese was known as a commercial fishing stronghold until fish catches declined. North Carolina statutes were amended so that the state-owned seafood park located there could become a marine park allowing other types of enterprises. Floating docks now reach into the harbor to accommodate charter boats. Boat storage is a big business with many fenced lots for boats and trailers and a large building seen here for an indoor dry stack option. (Francesca Beatrice Marie.)

Silver Lake Harbor in Ocracoke can add charter fishing vessels to its historical line-up of pirate boats, oceangoing schooners, and mullet skiffs. Captains take parties to the Pamlico Sound or offshore to the Gulf Stream. These kids had a great day of inshore Spanish mackerel fishing with Ronnie O'Neal in August 1990. Getting their photograph taken with the captain are, from left to right, David Bolanowski and friend from Camden, New Jersey, and Beach and Rheana Gray of Wanchese. (RWG.)

Maureen "Mo" Klause (right) of Ocean City, New Jersey, pictured here with mate Daniel Sheeler (left), holds 30 records in the International Game Fish Association database. As a fisherwoman, she seeks to catch the largest fish on the lightest tackle. She keeps her hobby affordable by fishing within driving distance of her home. A favorite spot of hers is Ocracoke, where she tracks the huge channel bass found there. (Maureen Klause.)

When world-record seeker Mo Klause fishes out of Ocracoke, she hires Ernie Doshier as her captain. Doshier sensitively handles his 25-foot privateer so that Klause can fight the fish with light tackle. She takes a conservationist stance and releases the fish she catches. With a light line, she gets a better perspective on fish behavior. She can feel it surface and dive and is even aware of it shaking its head. (Maureen Klause.)

Documenting a catch with an eye on a world record requires strict adherence to the rules, even though the program hinges on the honor system. The fish has to be weighed and measured on solid ground, and a photograph must be taken of the angler, the fish, and the rod and reel. On November 4, 2018, Mo Klause caught this International Game Fish Association record, a 40.5-pound channel bass on a four-pound test line. Mate Alan Doshier helped her keep the fish wet with minimal handling for release. (Maureen Klause.)

Sarah Gardner and her husband, Brian Horsley, were the first captains to take out fly-fishing clients from Oregon Inlet Fishing Center. Mastering the back-and-forth motion of a fly-fishing rod in a mountain stream has to be likened to an art form. Fly-fishing is more difficult on the Outer Banks due to wind, water depth, and tide. Sarah finds the challenge mentally engaging. She has attracted corporate sponsors who give her discounts on fishing gear to offset the couple's overhead. (Brian Horsley.)

Outdoors-minded Sarah Gardner has almost more interests than time. Not only does she guide fly-fishing trips from Oregon Inlet, Harkers Island, and Alaska, she leads turkey-hunting parties in Carteret County, bow hunts elk in Colorado, and teaches fishing school in the Bahamas. Sarah and her partner in adventure, Brian Horsley, use photography to document inland and offshore wildlife such as bluebirds, clapper rails, porpoise, sea turtles, and the endangered North Atlantic right whale. (Brian Horsley.)

A wide variety of clients, like the two pictured here, come from all over the world to fish with Sarah Gardner (center) and Brian Horsley of Outer Banks Fly Fishing. Their boats, *Flat Out* and *Fly Girl*, are docked next to *Miss Oregon Inlet II*, the headboat at Oregon Inlet Fishing Center. Sometimes for fun, Sarah will take a spin out on the headboat and act as mate. The bottom-fishing tourists have no idea that a world-renowned fisherwoman is helping them bait a hook. (Brian Horsley.)

Roy "Tripp" Phillips III got his captain's six-pack license at age 18 and obtained his 100-ton license a short time later. The owners of the *Miss Oregon Inlet* headboat offered him a job as captain in 2020 when he came home from college during the COVID-19 pandemic. When a customer asks, "Are you old enough to be to be running this thing?" Phillips replies, "No, but don't tell anyone." (Brian Horsley.)

Tripp Phillips (right) is pictured at age 14 in this photograph when he started on the *Miss Oregon Inlet* as a bait boy before working his way to mate. These days, as captain of the *Miss Oregon Inlet II*, Phillips and his crew give their fishing customers a lively time catching keepers such as croakers, grey trout, and sea mullet. The hardest aspect of his job is predicting and handling the weather. When he sees storm clouds building, he does not hesitate to radio the captains he respects for advice. (Brian Horsley.)

Lines were in and anticipation was high during the *Miss Oregon Inlet* Seventh Annual Youth Fishing Tournament in 2021, an event designed to build a love for fishing and respect for the water in children. Headboat co-owner and tournament coordinator Melodye Cannady Calloway wanted local children to experience the joys of being on the water like she did as the daughter of legendary captain Buddy Cannady. (Brian Horsley.)

This young angler with her fishing scorecard around her neck looked like she was on her way to a strong finish in the youth fishing tournament. A representative from North Carolina Marine Fisheries began the tournament with a talk about the importance of releasing small fish. At the conclusion of the day, each participant was given a medal and a brand-new rod and reel provided by Oregon Inlet Fishing Center. (Brian Horsley.)

The freckled arm holding a puffer fish belongs to retired Coastguardsman and prankster Edward Lee Mann. No doubt, Mann blew up this puffer like a balloon to amaze and delight the children aboard the *Miss Oregon Inlet*. The boat owners decided to replace the original wooden vessel after 44 years of service. A larger, more modern, fiberglass boat was purchased in Belmar, New Jersey, and became the *Miss Oregon Inlet II* in 2022. (Brian Horsley.)

Many boat owners seek to create new streams of revenue when they consider the expenses that come along with owning a boat. In June 1988, the *Crystal Dawn*, a headboat belonging to charter fisherman Allan Foreman and docked at Pirate's Cove, took a late afternoon sightseeing cruise on Roanoke Sound. The rowdy bunch of sightseers looked like they were contemplating jumping off the top of the cabin. (Drew Wilson Collection, OBHC.)

Fourteen-year-old Matthew Sphar of Attica, New York, prepares to cast a net for minnows along the marshy shallows of Oregon Inlet on July 21, 1993. The minnows that he and his father caught on the southern tip of Bodie Island would be used for a fishing expedition later that afternoon. Unlike many other beach destinations, visitors have access to wild spaces on the Outer Banks. (Drew Wilson Collection, OBHC.)

As the son of a National Park Service ranger, Michael Doll is careful not to incur any tickets by leaving a vehicle on park service land. He walks and wades to the flats around Bodie Island Lighthouse, his favorite trout spot. Doll carves, paints, constructs, and endlessly tweaks his own jointed trout lures. Even though he is a chef, he never cooks and eats what he catches but prefers to see the beautiful creatures swim away. (Michael Doll.)

Sean Reier (left) and Brian Winnett (right) were both living on the Outer Banks as National Park Service employees in 2015. They enjoyed fishing from kayaks for the opportunity to escape the crowds and visit parts of the islands that were inaccessible by land or deep-draft boats. They fished for whatever was around, which, on this day, was speckled trout. (Brian Winnett.)

On a slick calm day, the Bodie Island Lighthouse can be seen just above the toe of kayak fisherman Brian Winnett's left boot. Winnett described his love of kayak fishing: "When you see the marsh line and shoals change after each storm, you get an appreciation for how dynamic the barrier islands are. Since the fish can sort of pull you around in a kayak, you can be successful using lighter tackle which also increases the fun." (Brian Winnett.)

Two baseball greats, hitter Ted Williams (left) of Red Sox fame and pitcher James "Catfish" Hunter (right) of the New York Yankees, attended the 25th Annual Nags Head Surf Fishing banquet at the Carolinian Hotel on Saturday, October 11, 1975. As part of the tournament, avid fisherman Williams (who would later be inducted into the International Game Fish Association Hall of Fame) rode the beach with local radio reporter Ken Mann as they gave live coverage of the action. (Ken Mann.)

The Outer Banks Bass Masters Club organized a fishing tournament that took place in Kitty Hawk Bay in 1974. The club used this press kit photograph from the previous year as a promotional tool. At that time, bass fishing in the Currituck Sound and adjacent waters was top in the nation. Freshwater bass spawn on the sandy bottom near the Kitty Hawk shore or in sand flats in milfoil. (Ken Mann.)

In April 1967, Libby Creef of Manteo posed with a white perch from a freshwater canal in Southern Shores. Visitors usually associate Dare County with saltwater fishing, but largemouth bass, black bass, bream, and white perch can be caught in the fresh sounds, lakes, and streams of the Dare coast from mid-spring until December. (Aycock Brown Collection, OBHC.)

Emma Daniels, 16 years old, of Wanchese, joined her father, Joey, in his passion for speargun fishing in the summer of 2019 and speared a sheepshead in the Roanoke Sound. Emma comes from a fishing family, and that, plus her love for the water, culminated in her desire to attend the US Merchant Marine Academy in Kings Point, New York. After graduation, she aspires to be the captain of a pilot boat that leads ships to port. (Joey Daniels.)

The dotted pattern emerging from the sand at the left was the debut of the Herbert C. Bonner Bridge. It would span Oregon Inlet and connect to the sand at the top right of this early-1960s aerial shot. The photograph illustrates a truth that is witnessed by those who fish the Outer Banks—that land, sound, inlet, sea, and sky meld together into one awe-inspiring scape. (Creef family.)

Susan Etheridge (left) and Nettie Brown (right) hold a tuna as a photograph prop in the mid-1970s. Susan is the daughter of fishing legend Willie Etheridge Jr., who brought the first blue marlin to Oregon Inlet Fishing Center. Nettie is the granddaughter of Aycock Brown, the photographer who made it his life's mission to promote Dare County with his pictures of pretty girls and fishing trophies. (Nettie Brown Tisch.)

DISCOVER THOUSANDS OF LOCAL HISTORY BOOKS FEATURING MILLIONS OF VINTAGE IMAGES

Arcadia Publishing, the leading local history publisher in the United States, is committed to making history accessible and meaningful through publishing books that celebrate and preserve the heritage of America's people and places.

Find more books like this at
www.arcadiapublishing.com

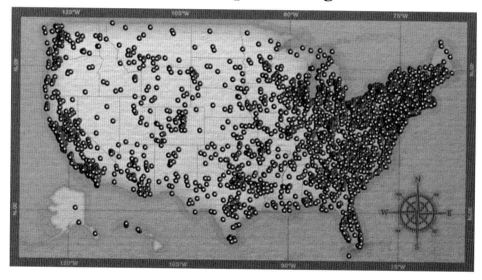

Search for your hometown history, your old stomping grounds, and even your favorite sports team.

Consistent with our mission to preserve history on a local level, this book was printed in South Carolina on American-made paper and manufactured entirely in the United States. Products carrying the accredited Forest Stewardship Council (FSC) label are printed on 100 percent FSC-certified paper.

MADE IN THE